Darussalam International Publications Limited

Office : 0208 539 4885
Fax: 020 8181 6544
Web : www.darussalam.com
Email : info@darussalam.com

Prinded by Mega Printing in Turkey

LIFE:
ITS SIGNIFICANCE AND LEVELS

Written by Ibn Qayyim al-Jawziyyah
Translated by Abdul Ali Hamid

FOREWORD

This is a very valuable piece of writing by the famous scholar Ibn Qayyim al-Jawziyyah (d. 751 AH), which deals with the significance of life. He explains that there are various levels of life: one of which is where we live in this world with all other creatures. This life is very short and temporary. Beyond this life is another permanent life which is not going to end. He tells his readers what is going to happen in that life. The people will be treated in that life according to their performance in this worldly life. This life is the place of work and the next one is the place of accounting and getting the result. It is only the people who have faith in Allah ﷻ and His Messenger ﷺ who understand this matter and strive to achieve the pleasure of Allah ﷻ. They will enjoy the life in the Hereafter, which will offer them all kinds of pleasure - which no eye has ever seen, no ear has ever heard of and no mind has ever thought of.

Unfortunately many people are mindless of that life and pass their time in comfortable and sumptuous living in this life, believing that they are lucky or that what they have is solely due to their efforts. Their selfish indulgence in this life does not allow them time to consider the next. They will later regret this, when they face the consequences of their deeds and wish to be sent back to the world in order to do something better or different with the time they were granted. Allah ﷻ gave them enough time to carry out His commands and His Messenger ﷺ explained everything in detail, but Satan had hold of them and misguided them.

The author explains everything and urges people to pay heed to the life to come. He also describes other beings, such as the life of the angels, the soul after it leaves the body and so on. He cements his arguments by citations from the Qur'an and the sayings of the Messenger of Allah ﷺ.

This section about life is extracted from his book *Madarij al-Salikin*, which is a lengthy book dealing with the stages of Sufism. This treatise is extracted from it and although it is small in size it contains very important messages for the believers. The book is written in Arabic but seeing its importance I decided to present it to the readers in the English language, hoping that Allah ﷻ will help them to understand and follow the right path.

I would like to extend my sincere gratitude to Brother R. Farooq, Project Co-Ordinator at Al-Nasr Trust. I would like also to thank my friend Khalid Mehr, the Director of the Trust, who introduced me to Brother Farooq. May Allah ﷻ give them full reward for their help and support.

Abdul Ali Hamid
Slough, Berks, SL1 3PP
E-mail: aahamid@hotmail.com

LIFE: ITS SIGNIFICANCE AND LEVELS
By Ibn Qayyim al-Jawziyyah

Allah, the Most Glorious, says:
"Is one who was dead and We gave him life and made for him light with which to walk among people, comparable to someone trapped in deep darkness who cannot escape?" *(6: 122)*

The meaning of this verse is that a man whose heart was devoid of the spirit of knowledge, guidance and faith was given the spirit by Almighty Allah. This spirit breathed life into his heart with the recognition of His unity, His knowledge and His love and devotion to His worship alone. It is for this reason Allah, the Most High, describes those who lack this spirit as dead. He says:
"Is one who was dead and We gave him life." *(6: 122)*

He also says:
"You cannot make the dead hear, nor can you make deaf hear the call." *(27: 80)*

Almighty Allah describes His revelation as a spirit because it gives life to hearts and souls. He says:
"So We have revealed a spirit to you by Our command: you knew neither the scripture nor the faith, but We made it a light, guiding with it whoever We will of Our servants." *(42: 52)*

Allah Almighty says the Qur'an is a spirit, which gives life and is a light that produces illumination.

He also says:
"He sends down angels with inspiration at His command, to whichever of His servants He chooses, to give His warning: 'There is no deity except Me, so fear Me.'" *(16: 2)*

He also says:
"He is exalted in rank, the Lord of the Throne. He sends the revelation with His teachings to whichever of His servants He will, in order to warn of the Day of Meeting." *(40; 15)*

So, the revelation is the life of the spirit and that spirit is the life of the body. Whoever is deprived of this spirit has missed the purpose of life in this world and the Hereafter. In this world, he lives like animals in a life of hardship, and in the Hereafter he will go to Hell where he will not die or live.

Allah, the Most Glorious, has reserved a good life for the people who know Him, love Him and are dedicated to Him. He said:
"Whoever does good deeds, whether male or female, and has faith, We will give good life and reward them according to the best of their actions." *(16: 97)*

"Good life" has been explained as producing satisfaction, contentment, good provision and so on. The correct interpretation is that it refers to the life and pleasure of the heart and its delight and happiness with belief and recognition of Allah ﷻ, as well as His love, turning to Him, and putting trust in Him. There is no more pleasant life than this, which the believer may enjoy, and there is no higher comfort than this, except for the comfort of Paradise. Some people of knowledge used to say: "There are periods that I have experienced, in which I have said, 'If the people of Paradise are in this situation, then they truly have a comfortable life.'"

Another person said: "There are times in which the heart dances in ecstasy."

When the life of the heart is good, the life of the rest of the body will be equally as good. For this reason Allah ﷻ made the painful life, which is the opposite of the peaceful life, for those who turn away from His remembrance and guidance.

This blissful life is in all three abodes, i.e. in this world, in the *Barzakh* and in the final abode. In the same way the stressful life is in all three abodes. The righteous people are in happiness here and there and the wicked are in Hell here and there. Allah, the Most High, explains it by saying:
"There is good in this present world for those who do good deeds, but their home in the Hereafter is far better." *(16: 30)*

The Almighty also says:
"Ask your Lord for forgiveness, then turn back to Him. He will grant you wholesome enjoyment until an appointed time, and give His grace to everyone who has merit." *(11: 3)*

It shows that the remembrance of Allah the Exalted, and love, obedience and devotion to Him are sufficient guarantee for the most blissful life in this world and the Hereafter. To turn away from Him and forget and disobey Him will result in a measurable life in this world and the Hereafter.

The author of *al-Manazil* said:
"Life in this part indicates three matters: The first life is the life of knowledge from the death of ignorance. It has three phases: phase of fear, phase of hope and phase of love."

His statement "life in this part" refers to the special life, which is discussed among the mystics, not the common life shared by all living creatures - the living beings and the plants. Life has various levels, which are mentioned below:

1. Life of earth
The first level is the life of the earth with plants. Allah the Exalted says:
"Allah sends water down from the sky and with it revives the earth after it is dead. There truly is a sign in this for people who listen." *(16: 65)*

He says about water:
"We gave with water life to a land that was dead." *(50: 11)*
"We send down pure water from the sky, so that We can revive a dead land with it." *(25: 48, 49)*

The Almighty made in this life a proof of the life after the Resurrection. This life is a real one at this level, used in every language and spoken of by all the people. A poet says, praising Abd al-Muttalib:
'With Shaybat al-Hamd Allah gave life to our land when we had no water and rain failed to come.'

2. Life of growth
The second level is the life of growth and nourishment. This life is shared by plants and living creatures who survive on food. Allah Almighty says:
"We made every living thing from water." *(21: 30)*

The jurists have two different opinions concerning the issue of perception/sensitivity/perceptive faculty and whether it is affected by life.

The correct view is that perception has a life of growth and nourishment and not of sense and movement. It therefore does not become impure by death. If loss of growth and nourishment resulted in impurity, the plants and trees would become impure when they lose their lives. Based on this, the general body of scholars agrees that perception does not become polluted by death.

3. Life of a living creature
The third level is the life of a living creature, which takes more than is required for its growth and nourishment. That is its sense and movement. It is affected by the painful conditions and loss of contact and so on. This life is above the life of plants, and it becomes strong and weak in one living creature according to its conditions. Its life after birth is more perfect than when it was in the womb of its mother, and its life while it is healthy and sound is better than when it is ill and unhealthy. This life differs greatly in various situations; hence the life of a snake is more perfect than the life of a mosquito. Whoever contests it, is challenging common sense and intelligence.

4. The life of angels and soul

The fourth level is the life of the living creatures that are not nurtured with food and drink, such as the angels and the soul when it parts from the body. Their life is higher than the living creatures that live on food and drink. They do not suffer from tiredness and fatigue, nor are they overtaken by sleep or experience exhaustion. Allah, the Most High said about the angels: **"They glorify (Allah) night and day and do not slacken."** *(21: 20)*

In the same way when souls get rid of the bodies and are freed, they obtain a new life, which is more pleasant than this one, if it was prosperous with good deeds. However, if it was wretched, it will suffer from the torment.

5. Life of knowledge

The fifth level is the life of knowledge from the death of ignorance. Ignorance is death for its people. This is stated in the following lines:
'Ignorance is death for a person before physical death, and their body become their grave. Their soul feels strange in their body and they will not be raised until the Day of Resurrection.'

An ignorant man is dead of heart and soul, although he has life in his body. His body is a grave, which he carries on the earth. Allah, the Glorious and the Exalted said:
"Is a dead person brought back to life by Us, and given light with which to walk among people, comparable to someone trapped in deep darkness who cannot escape?" *(6: 122)*

"This is a revelation, an illuminating Qur'an to warn anyone who is truly alive, so that Allah's verdict may be passed against the disbelievers." *(36: 69-70.)*

The Almighty also said:
"You cannot make the dead hear and you cannot make the deaf hear your call" *(30: 52)*

"Allah makes anyone He wills hear (His message). You cannot make those in their graves hear." *(35: 22)*

Because of the death of their hearts Allah compared them with the people in graves. These people's souls are dead and their bodies are graves for them. As the people of the graves cannot hear, these people also cannot hear. Life means sensation and movement and since these hearts do not have the sense of knowledge and belief and do not act according to them, they are dead in real sense. It is not like the death of the body, but is the death of the heart and the soul.

In his book *al-Zuhd*, Imam Ahmad quoted Luqman's advice to his son saying:
'My son, keep the company of learned people and keep your knees closer to them. Allah gives the hearts life by the light of wisdom as He revives the earth with heavy rain.'

Mu'adh ibn Jabal said:
"Acquire knowledge. Its acquisition produces fear of Allah. Its search is worship, engagement in its discussion is glorification and endeavour in seeking it is jihad. Its teaching to those who have no knowledge is charity and passing it to its people is an act of reward. By it the lawful and forbidden matters are known and the paths of the people of Paradise are found. It is the companion in loneliness, a friend in solitariness and a source of conversation in solitude. It is a guide to ease and hardship, a weapon against the enemies and a source of happiness with friends. Allah raises by it some people and makes them leaders of good, whose examples are followed, their actions are imitated and their opinions are accepted. Angels wish to be their companions and cover them with their wings. Every fresh and withered plant seeks forgiveness for them. The fish and insects of the sea and the beasts and cattle of the land pray for them. This is because they have knowledge, which gives life to the heart and prevents ignorance, and is a lamp for eyes in the darkness. Through knowledge a man reaches the levels of the righteous people and achieves the highest rank in the world and the Hereafter. To contemplate on it is equal to fasting, and studying it is equal to keep a night vigil. Through it the lawful and forbidden are known. It is the head of the deeds, which are subordinate to it. The fortunate ones are granted it and the unfortunate are deprived of it."

The above statement is cited by al-Tabarani and Ibn Abd al-Barr and others. It is attributed to the Messenger ﷺ but this is incorrect.

6. Life of intention and resolution
The sixth level is the life of intention and ambition. The weakness of intention and endeavour is caused by the weakness of the heart. The more energetic the heart is, the higher its ambition will be and stronger its discretion and love will be. It leads to the freedom of the heart from any obstacle, which may weaken its intention. Weakness of endeavour and slackness of ambition are caused by two things: lack of perception and sense, or the existence of the obstacle that has reduced the energy. Strength of perception and power of intention are the signs of the strength of life, and their weakness is the indication of life's weakness. High ambition and sincerity of intention and endeavour lead to the most perfect and noble life. Good life can be achieved through high ambition, sincere love and pure intention. A good life will be in accordance with the degree of sincerity. A person with a measurable life is one who has low ambition in seeking Allah the Almighty's pleasure and weak love and resolution. The life of the animals is better than his life. It is said in the lines of a poem:
"Your day, O deceived, is passed in negligence and heedlessness, and your night is spent in sleeping. Certainly the death is going to take you. You endeavour for things, the result of which you will regret. This is how the animals live in this world. You feel happy with what is going to end, and rejoice in wishes like a person who is deceived by pleasures in a dream."

The point is that the life of the heart revolves around knowledge, intention and ambition. When

people watch such a person, they say: he possesses a living heart. Life of the heart depends on consistent remembrance of Allah, and abandoning the sins. Abdullah ibn al-Mubarak has explained it in the following lines:
"I noticed that sins cause death to the heart; if a person continues in committing them, he faces humiliation. Avoiding sins gives life to the heart, and it is better for you than to disobey your soul. Religion was corrupted by kings, evil Rabbis and Priests. They sold their souls and got no profit through their sales. These people devour rotten material, the loss of which is obvious for a man of intelligence."

I heard Shaykh al-Islam Ibn Taymiyyah saying that if a person regularly says the following between the Sunnah and the Fardh of the dawn prayer forty times, Allah will give life to his heart:

يا حي يا قيوم لا إله إلا أنت   'O Ever-Living, O Sustainer, there is no god except You'.

As Allah the Exalted has given life to the body through food and drink, He has given life to the heart through regular remembrance, turning to Allah and avoiding sins. Negligence and interest in evil deeds and lust weaken the heart. This weakness continues affecting it until it dies. The sign of its death is that it is unable to recognise the good and bad.

Abdullah ibn Mas'ud asked his followers: "Do you know who the person of dead heart is? He is the one about whom it is said: 'The one who died and was in peace is not dead, the dead is that who is living.'" His followers asked him who that person was and he replied: "He is the one who does not know the difference between good and bad."

The perfect man is one who is scared of his heart's death and not his body's. The majority of people are afraid of the death of their bodies and they do not care about their hearts' death. They know only one life, and that is physical life. This is the result of the death of the heart and the soul. This physical life is similar to passing shade, quickly drying plants and dreams, which seem real. When the person wakes up he realises that it was mere imagination. It was well explained by 'Umar ibn Abd al-Aziz who said:
'If the life of the world from the beginning to the end was given to a man when death came to him, he would be like a man who saw in his dream what pleased him. On awakening he would have nothing in his hand.'

It is said:
"Death is of two types: the death of intention and physical death. The physical death is life for he whose intentions are dead."

The meaning of this statement is that the intentional death is to suppress the destructive desires and quench their burning fires and control their devastating lusts. When that is done the person's heart and soul become free to think about matters in which lie his perfection and success. He realises that preference of quickly passing shade over permanent, excellent life is the greatest loss. When desires are left to intrude and the soul takes control, then the heart becomes either disgraced, captive or defeated and expelled from its place and its abode, which is the only the source of comfort for a person. Alternatively, it is killed without feeling the pain of injury. The best condition for him is to be in a tussle, winning and being defeated. When a person dies his natural death, his soul lives because of the useful knowledge, good deeds and the superior conditions he acquired. His life is in accordance with his intentional death in this world.

This is a subject that only people of intelligence and discretion can understand, and only people of high ambitions and those with pure souls can follow it.

7. Life of good conduct

The seventh level is the life of good conduct and praiseworthy qualities. It is a well established life for a person. He need not struggle in the stages of perfection, and it is not difficult for him to reach it. His good conduct and qualities are essential parts of him, to the extent that if he were to abandon them, he would be parting with what is his nature and character. The life of a person for whom modesty, chastity, generosity, ideal character, truthfulness and faithfulness are inherent in him is superior to the life of the one who forces himself and struggles to acquire them. The latter is like a man who is affected by the causes of disease and tries to treat them by their opposites, while the former is free from it.

The more these characters are perfect in a person, the more his life will be complete and powerful. This is how the quality of modesty (*haya'*) was derived from life (*hayah*) in both word and meaning. The most perfect person in life is one who is the most perfect in modesty. On the other hand the lack of modesty in a person is the result of deficiency in his life. This is because when the soul is dead, it does not feel the pain of evil acts, and does not feel shame for them. If it is full of life, it feels it and is ashamed of it. In the same way all the praiseworthy characters and noble qualities are subject to the power of life, and they are reduced according to the lack of it. The life of a courageous person is more superb than the life of a cowardly man, and the life of a generous persona is better than the life of a miserly person. The life of an intelligent and shrewd man is incomparable with a dull and stupid person. This shows why the Prophets ﷺ were perfect in their lives, to the extent that the power of their lives prevented the earth from affecting their bodies. They were superior of all people in moral conduct. Then the people who followed them were like them. Now compare the life of worthless swearer, scorner, slander-monger, hinderer of good, transgressor, sinner and an imposter with the life of a generous, brave, kind, just, decent and charitable person. You will find the first dead compared to the second one. How correct is the saying of someone:
'There is no good in the life of a person if he is counted among the waste.'

8. Life of Happiness

The eighth level of life is the life of happiness and delight and joy with Allah Almighty. This comes after achieving the goal, which brings joy to the person. There is no benefit in life without it. This is the life that is sought by almost everyone, but they missed the way and took the wrong path. All the people struggled to acquire that life but most of them were deprived of it. The cause of their deprivation was the lack of intelligence and discretion and weakness of ambition and resolution. This is due to the fact that its essence is sharp insight and critical judgement. Insight is similar to being blind, or suffering the loss of one eye, bleariness or inflammation, whereas some eyes can see perfectly in light and brightness. These diseases may occur from birth or can be caused later on in life.

The point is that this level of life is the highest one, but how can a man reach it when his reason is captivated by vain desires and his intention is restricted to acquire sensual delight? He has the worst manners and his religion is covered with sins and violations. Lowly matters arrest his ambition and his belief is not derived from the lamp of the Prophecy.

He is deeply engrossed in vain desires, bending on doubts and does not listen to good advice. He objects to those who want to guide him. He is heedless of the lasting pleasures and his heart wanders in every valley. If he could rid his soul of these dictations, keep away from the company of his evil companions, get out of the confinement of ignorance to the open space of knowledge, move away from the prison of the desires to that of guidance and from the impurity of the soul to the purity of sacred sanctuary – if he could only do this, he would witness the love with which he had grown. In addition, he will gain more power through this and will be honoured among his people. It will remove the speck in the eyes of his insight, and will redeem him from a dangerous disease, which could lead to his death.

If you say that you mentioned an unfamiliar life among the living dead ones, can you then describe its quality so that I may be able to taste it? Now it is clear to me that the life we are living is worse than the life of the animals because the life of the animals is free from abominations and loathsome elements.

I will reply that by Allah, your longing for this life and interest in seeking knowledge about it is evidence that you are alive and not dead.

Begin by recognising Allah ﷻ and find the way to Him. He will help you achieve it and will destroy the darkness of the ill disposition through rays of insight. As a result your heart will correctly repent and carry out open and secret commands and refrain from the open and secret prohibitions. It will guard your heart and will not allow any thought that Allah does not like or any useless notion to penetrate. In this way the heart will be free to be devoted to the remembrance of Allah ﷻ and to be involved in love and devotion to Him. It will provide it with an opportunity to rid its confinement of the soul, and to be alone with the Lord, and engage in His remembrance.

It is said by some poets: "I depart from the house so that I speak to my soul alone in secret'"

When it happens, his heart and thoughts will focus on seeking his Lord and longing towards Him. If he is true in it, he will gain the love of the Messenger ﷺ and his spiritual power will dominate his heart. The Prophet ﷺ will become his leader, teacher, master and an ideal for him as Allah made His Prophet a guide to Him. He should read his life's accounts and the way he received the revelation. He should study his characters, conducts, manners, his movements, sleeping and waking up, his worship and his treatment of his family and his companions and indeed all those around him. It will lead him to feel as though he is with him as a member of the Companions.

If this takes root in his heart, the door of understanding of the revealed message will be opened for him. When he reads a chapter of the Qur'an, his heart will perceive the purpose of it and the situation about which it was revealed. He will notice his own bad and abominable characteristics and will struggle to free himself from it, as though struggling to be cured from a dangerous disease. He will be able to see praiseworthy deeds and characters and will try to acquire them.

When he is able to consolidate it, another eye will open in his heart by which he will visualize the attributes of Allah the Almighty. His heart will be able to conceive them as though he sees them through his eyes. He will reach such a high stage, that he will witness Allah the Almighty above the creatures, established on His Throne. He controls the affairs of His kingdom from there, speaks to His chosen people through revelation. He addresses His slave Gabriel and dispatches him with whatsoever He wants to whomsoever He wishes of His servants. The affairs are taken up and presented to Him.

His heart will witness a powerful Lord who issues commands and prohibitions, sends His messengers, reveals books and is worshipped alone. He has no partner, no match and no equal. No one has any power in the administration of the affairs; He alone takes care of His kingdom. In this stage the person will witness his Lord having full power and authority. Nothing can move or halt without His permission. No one can bring benefit or cause harm, give or withhold, give abundance or hold back without His order. He will be able to conceive that all matters are under His power and He stands alone and administers the affairs of His creatures.

When he reaches this stage, he will witness the attributes that complete all the qualities of perfection of life and those which produce the perfection of hearing seeing, having power, will, speech and all other qualities. Then there is the quality of the Eternal, which puts everything in order. So, the Living, the Eternal is the One who has all the qualities of perfection and He does what He wills.

After that comes the stage of closeness and companionship. He feels that He, the Exalted, is with him, not away from him, though He is above the heavens on His Throne. He is apart from His creatures and carries out the creation, management and command. He will gain intimacy with Him with glorification and honour. He will feel close to Him after being lonely, gain power after being feeble, be delighted after being sad and receive blessings after he was deprived. Now he will understand the meaning of His statement:
"My worshipper continues to come near Me with voluntary works until I love him. When I love him, I become his ear with which he listens, his eye by which he sees, his hand by which he holds and his leg with which he walks. If he asks Me for anything, I will surely grant him, and if he seeks protection, I will definitely give him protection."

No doubt that this person's life is the most pleasant one. He loves Allah ﷻ and is loved by Him; he is close to Him and He is near him. Allah the Almighty became his beloved because of the domination of His thought over his heart. He is engaged in His remembrance and is putting his effort to achieve His pleasure. Allah becomes his ears, eyes, hands and legs. These are his tools for moving and working. Through this favour when he hears, he hears by his beloved; when he sees, he sees by Him; when he holds, he holds by Him and when he walks, he walks by Him.

If you find it difficult to understand how a lover will hear, see, hold and walk by his beloved when He is not with him, disregard it and leave the matter to those who belong to this field. 'Leave the love for the people who are known by it; they suffered from love until it became easy for them.'

The intention of the traveller to his Lord is focused on two things: to exert himself to meet his love true and to endeavour to follow His commands. He does not cease in this effort until the signs of His recognition appear and the indications of His names and attributes are noticeable on him. These signs are hidden from him sometimes and are visible sometimes. They appear with benevolence and disappear through slackness. These periods of apathy are inevitable for the worshipper. Every worker has enthusiasm and every enthusiasm faces laxity. The highest laxity is that of revelation which belongs to the prophets. Then there is the laxity of special conditions belonging to those who recognise Allah. Then comes the slackness of intention, which belongs to the seekers, and lastly comes the slackness of deeds, which is for the worshippers. In these periods of slackness there is a variety of wisdom and mercy. They provide an opportunity to know the Divine qualities and acknowledge His favours. They also enhance interest in the bounty and a struggle to achieve it. These evidences appear again and again and increase until they settle down in the heart and colour it completely. In this condition the slackness does not affect the servant but becomes a favour, a comfort and a source of relaxation.

When the soul of the lover is attached to his beloved, he struggles to increase it and develop its power. After that he works to acquire the love of his beloved for him. However, it does not destroy the first attempt but is incorporated in the second one and he becomes concerned with both. The stage of being 'his ears with which he hears and his eyes with which he sees' is connected with this second endeavour. He struggles to approach his Lord in order to safeguard his love and acquire His love for him.

Now he becomes more energetic in achieving the love of his beloved by all sorts of good deeds. His heart becomes engaged in love, repentance, trust, fear and hope. His tongue is busy in remembrance and recitation of the speech of his beloved, and his limbs in carrying out His orders. He does not slacken in struggle to come closer to Him.

This is the march to the goal and cannot be attained without it. This objective can only be reached through a certain gate and a certain way. This way brings to him all the different aspects of the journey: the presence, the awe, vigilance and removal of the thoughts and clearance of the inner side.

First of all, the lover start with external deeds of approach, then he proceeds to the stage of being close. This means to be attracted to the beloved by all: his soul, heart, reason and body. This leads to the stage of *ihsan* (sincerity), and he is able to worship Allah as though he sees Him. In this stage he utilizes the powers of his heart: love, repentance, magnification, respect and fear. This causes the generosity of spending the soul and he is ready to sacrifice everything for the love of his beloved. He surrenders his soul, spirit, intention and all his deeds to his beloved instantly without any effort. If it is attained then the lover has succeeded in gaining the stage of closeness and its secrets. However, if it is not so then his effort was only outwardly, by the tongue and body. He is required to continue the struggle by remembrance and good deeds regularly. Hopefully he may reach the closeness he wishes to attain.

Behind this inner closeness there is another thing. There is no more beautiful expression of it than what related by the Almighty:
"If my worshipper comes close to Me by a span of the hand, I come to him by the length of an arm. If he approaches Me by an arm's length, I come to him by the span of the outstretched arms. If he comes to Me walking, I come to him running."

The lover gets the real taste of this message. The Almighty mentioned three stages of closeness and alluded to the ones below and above them. He mentioned the nearness of the worshipper by the span of a hand and His approach to him by the length of an arm. When the worshipper realises this closeness he moves to the closeness of an arm length, and he feels the approach of the Lord to him by outstretched arm.

When he gets the sweetness of this nearness, he speeds up to his Lord, and realises His coming to him running. This is where the Prophetic statement ends, indicating that when the Lord's worshipper hurries to Him, His speed will be faster than his running to Him. The Prophet ﷺ stopped at this point, either because of the greatness of the reward or because it is a reward which no ear has heard of and no human mind has thought of. Alternatively, he referred to the preceding stages as though to say, judge the rest by them. In comparison of your effort to approach to your Lord, He will do more. It shows the degree of the approach of Allah to the servant. When a servant approaches to his beloved with soul and all his powers, intention, statements and deeds, the Lord will come nearer to him in proportion to his closeness to Him. Closeness in all matter is not a physical closeness, but a real one, because the Lord Almighty is above the heavens on His Throne and the servant is on earth.

This place is the secret of the spiritual path and essence of servitude. It is the sense of reaching, which the people of spiritual effort talk about. The essential part of it is the intention of coming close, and then approaching Him, which will lead to the condition of closeness, which means fully turning to the beloved.

The essence of this effort is that you sacrifice your desire for His will and be satisfied with what He grants you. What you get should be your exclusive share and desire. You may have already been told that anyone who approaches his beloved will in return get much more than he has given. You will also have learned that the highest standard of coming close is the total surrender of the servant, by his outward and inward, and by his existence, to his beloved. When a person does this, he has offered everything to Him; nothing was left for anyone else. If a devotee who approaches the Almighty through good deeds is given many times more, what do you think about a lover who approaches Him with his soul and all his eagerness, ambition, deeds and statements? This person has sacrificed himself for his beloved, so he deserves to be shown appreciation. He deserves to have his Lord, the Exalted, as his share and portion as a full reward. This is because the compensation is similar to the work. There are many evidences for it.

a. One of them is saying of Allah, the Glorious:
"Whosoever is mindful of Allah, He will make for him a way out, and will provide him from where he does not expect. And whoever puts his trust in Allah, He is sufficient for him."
(65: 2-3)

As you can see, the Almighty has differentiated between two rewards and made the reward of the one who puts his trust in Him being enough and sufficient for him.

b. When a martyr offers his life for the sake of Allah, He gives him a better and more superior life in His presence according to His honour.

c. When a person gives out something for the sake of Allah, He compensates him with better than that.

d. Allah, the Exalted, says:
"Remember Me, I will remember you; be grateful to Me and never be ungrateful." *(2: 152)*

e. The Almighty said in a qudsi Hadith:
"Whoever remembers Me in his mind, I will remember him in My mind, and if he remembers Me in a group, I will remember him in a better group."

f. He, the Most High, said:
"When a person comes close to Me by a span of the hand, I will come close to him by a an outstretched arm."

The worshipper in this way always gets in return better than what he has offered to his Lord. The one who strives to approach Allah with all his heart, soul and deeds, his Lord will grant him a life that is not matched with the variety of life the people have. His life compared with the life of unfortunate ones is like the life of the foetus with the life of the people of the world and the pleasure they have. The life of the lover of Allah is far better than these people's lives.

This is a sample of the description of this life and its merits. If the knowledge of it entails a pleasant life for the man, then what will be the case when the heart is absorbed in it and becomes a permanent condition of it? Only Allah's help is to be sought.

This life is the life of this world with its pleasure, if a person misses it, he very likely to miss the natural life. The real life is the life of lovers who find comfort in their beloved. Their souls receive peace with them, their hearts feel tranquility and they find rest with them and enjoy their love. There is emptiness in the heart, which can be filled only with the love of Allah Almighty and turning to Him completely. The heart can be put in order with it. If a person does not get it, his life will be filled with worries, grief, pain and regrets. If he is a man of high ambition, his soul will be shattered in the world because he will not accept something lesser. But if he is a man of low status, his life will be like the life of the most measurable animal. As a matter of fact the hearts cannot find peace except in the love of the first beloved. It is said in the lines of poetry: "Move your heart in love wherever you like, the love belongs to the first beloved. How many places a man stays on earth, but his yearning is for the first place."

9. The Life of the souls

The ninth level of the life is the life of the souls after parting from the bodies and getting release from this prison and its limitations. Beyond this world there is open space, comfort, rest and ease. This world in connection to the next one is like the womb of the mother in

connection to this world, or even less than that. Some spiritual leaders have said:
"Let your enthusiasm in getting out of the world be like your zeal for getting out of the narrow prisons and meeting your friends in beautiful gardens."

Allah, the Most High, said:
"If he is one of those who are brought near to Allah, he will have rest, ease and the garden of bliss." *(56: 88-89)*

The excellence of this life is in meeting the High Companion, and parting from the hurtful and wicked companions, the very sight of whom spoils the pleasure of life, let alone to mix and live with him. The lucky one will move towards the Sublime Companion among the people who have earned the favour of Allah: the messengers, the truthful ones, the martyrs and righteous ones, and they are the best companions. They will be blessed in the closeness of the Lord, the Most Beneficent, the Most Merciful.

A poet says:
"I said when they went to extreme in praise of life: death has thousands of merits which are not known. One of them is to meet Him in safety, and to part from a companion who is not just."

Had death been nothing better than a door to this life, and a bridge to cross to it, it would have been enough as a gift for the believer.

In another couplet of poetry:
"May Allah bless death because it is the most kind and gentle to us. It relieves the souls from pain and brings closer to the house which is more honourable."

Struggle in this short life, working hard and bearing trouble, are all for that life. All the knowledge and deeds are means to it. It is wakefulness and the life before it is sleep. It is real and the earlier life is a shadow. It is a life that combines the loss of the hateful and receiving of the lovable in a place where there is company and Divine presence. In it no desire is difficult to achieve and no desirable thing is missed. There is peace, rest, happiness and delight. Nobody can describe its essence; it is in a place we have not seen and we have not known its residents. The soul, because of staying in and being familiar with this narrow prison for long time, dislikes moving to the other world, and feels distressed with the idea of parting from it.

The news of this life reached us through the information of the Almighty, through the most perfect man who had the most accurate knowledge of his Lord. He was the most devoted person to Him. Its evidences were established in the hearts of the believing people as if they could see them with their eyes. As a result, their souls ran away from this transitory shadow and from a life mixed with all sorts of troubles and sufferings. They longed for the other life and that realm. They were filled with the passion of that pleasure and yearning, for the comforting breeze coming from the place of permanent bliss.

By Allah, a man who travelled to the land of justice, abundance, peace and happiness, leaving those who remained behind at a time when he was in need of them, and who responded to the caller when he called: "Hasten to success" is a lucky one. He sacrificed his soul to acquire the pleasure and gratification of the beloved. He continued his journey day and night and appreciated his walk after arrival. This is how a traveller in the night appreciates his travels in the morning.

It is not, by Allah, hard and difficult in this short life, which is like an hour of the day in comparison to the other. Allah, the Most High, said:
"It will seem to them that they lingered no more than a single hour of a day." *(46: 35)*

"On the Day He will gather them together, it will be as if they have stayed (in the world) no longer than a single hour, and they will recognise one another." *(10: 45)*

"It will be on the Day they see it, as though they had not remained (in the world) except for an afternoon or a morning." *(79: 46)*

"On the Day the Hour comes, the guilty will swear they remained no more than an hour." *(30: 55)*

"He will say, 'How many years were you on earth?' And they will reply, 'We stayed a day or a part of a day, but ask those who keep count.' He will say, 'You stayed but a little, if you had only known.'" *(23: 112-114)*

If one of us was to be dragged on his face, avoiding the thorns and stones of this life, it would still be very little and we would not have saved much.

What a pity for those that witnessed these two lives as they are and then took preference of the lower over the higher. It is only by the help of the One who holds the affairs in His hand. In His hand is the beginning and end of everything. He prevented the unfortunate ones from travelling to that house and attracted the hearts of those for whom the best reward is decided. He kept them on the right path, and made it easy for them to face the dangers. One group wasted the stages of their lives with those who remained behind and the other group spent their lives with those who went ahead. In the dust and smoke both groups are hidden, but very soon the dust will clear and those who did good deeds will be successful, and those who followed falsehood will lose.

The Prophet ﷺ described the pleasure and delight of that life. He said:
"No soul which has deposited good deeds with Allah will wish to return to the world and gain its treasure, except the martyr. He will wish to come back to the world because of the honour he received from Allah."

He wishes to return to the world in order to be killed again.

A spiritual leader heard someone singing the following:
"Life is the physical delight; this is what the philosopher says. Both a stupid and intelligent one takes the cup of death. Then the stupid goes under ground like the intelligent one. Ask the ground whether the clear question removed the doubt and suspicion."

The spiritual leader said: "May Allah destroy this man! How opposed he is to religion and reason! He is the enemy of instinct, Shari'ah, reason, faith and wisdom. Poor man! Because death does not distinguish between the good and bad, learned and ignorant, and all of them are buried in the ground, does it mean that all of them will be equal in the end? Some people travel from one town to another together but when they reach their destination they dwell in different places and are treated differently - are they equal? Each group has a place suitable for them. One is treated in a way opposite of what the other is. When these people arrive in the city some of them are lodged in its gardens, palaces and excellent places, and others are housed on the roads amongst the dogs. Aren't they from the same mother, but that one of them reached power and sovereignty and the other imprisonment and trouble?

You say to ask the earth about them. We did and it replied that it had only the disintegrated bodies and parts. It did not have their disbeliefs and beliefs, or their family honour and ranks, or their reason and stupidity, or their obedience and disobedience, or their certainty and doubt, or their belief in oneness and association, or their injustice and fairness or their knowledge and ignorance. This is what the earth said about the decayed corpses and disintegrated parts, saying that this is the news of what I have.

As for what happened to the souls, ask the books of the Lord of the universe, His truthful Messengers and their successors. Ask the Qur'an which has the certain information. Turn to the one who brought this book; he is the best to know it. Refer to knowledge and faith, as they are accepted witnesses. Ask the reasons and discretions because they have the real information.

"Do those who commit evil deeds think that We will deal with them in the same way as those who believe and do righteous deeds, that they will be alike in their living and their dying? How badly they judge! *(45: 21)*

Allah, who is the best Judge, is above this type of thought and assumption which suit only the greatest ignorant."

The spiritual person further said: The people who deal with this matter are of two kinds: A man who looks at the matters and another who looks into them. The former is bewildered because their shapes, designs and forms take hold of his senses and mind and scatter his thoughts and his heart. By looking at them with a physical eye he receives neither a lesson nor has the power of the selection. He misses the understanding and as a result he misses the full knowledge. On the other hand the man who looks in the matters, goes deeper from their forms to their realities and their purposes. He discovers the profound wisdom and full knowledge of their existence. He becomes capable of distinguishing between them and knows the harmful and profitable, right and wrong and the permanent and temporary, and is able to recognise the core from the shell. He develops the understanding of the means and the goals. He comes to realise that the world is the shell and the Hereafter is the core; the world is the place of sowing and the Hereafter is the place of harvesting. The world is transitory and the Hereafter is a lasting home.

When a person realises that the world is only a passage, he should become active in preparation of his lasting abode. He should understand that he was not brought to this world for staying forever, but for passing to another place, which will be his permanent abode. Mankind was preached about in every religion, at the tongue of every Prophet and by all evidences. Its signs were set and his departure was illustrated by examples. He was reminded of his birth and origin. All his affairs including his food and drink, and the heavens and the earth were explained. All the doubts were removed and the path was shown and the evidence was established. He was given a full opportunity to follow the right path. The man of right reason and correct insight became sure that departure from this place is a must and there is another place where he is destined to move to. This place has been prepared and for it he was created. He is definitely going there. This world is only a temporary hotel not a permanent home.

In fact whoever looks carefully in the existing materials of this world will come to realise that there is another world beyond this one, which is more perfect than this. This life compared to that is like sleep to wakefulness and like a shadow compared to the real object. He will perceive everything calling as his Lord and Creator has called:
"People, Allah's promise is true, so do not let the present life deceive you. Let not the Deceiver deceive you about Allah. *(35: 5)*

They call in silent language, which Allah spoke expressly:
"Tell them what the life of this world is like: We sent water down from the skies and the earth's vegetation absorbs it, but soon the plants turn to dry stubble scattered about by wind. Allah has power over everything." *(18: 45)*

"The example of this life is like the rain that We send down from the sky, which is absorbed by the plants of the earth, from which human and animals eat. But when the earth has taken on its finer appearance, and adorns itself, and its people think they have power over it, there comes Our command to it, by night or day, and We reduce it to stubble, as if it had not flourished just the day before. This is the way We explain the revelations for those who reflect." *(10: 24)*

"Bear in mind that the present life is just a game, a diversion, an attraction, a cause of boasting among you, of rivalry in wealth and children. It is like the rain whose (resulting) plants please the tillers, but then you see them wither away, turn yellow and become stubble. There is terrible punishment in the next life as well as forgiveness and approval from Allah. The life of this world is only an illusory pleasure." *(57: 20)*

Then Allah the Most Merciful encourages people to race to the next permanent world, which is not going to end:
"Race towards forgiveness from your Lord and a garden as wide as the heavens and the earth, prepared for those who believe in Allah and His messengers. That is the bounty of Allah, which He bestows on whoever He wills. Allah is the Possessor of great bounty. *(57:21)*

A spiritual man once heard the following lines of a Zindiq, namely Muhammad ibn Zakariyya the Physician, at the time of his death:
"Upon my life, I do not know now when the time of my departure has approached or where I am going. Where is the place of the soul after its skeleton has disintegrated form and decayed body?"

He said: "What are we going to do if he is unaware and does not know where he is heading to? We know where he and where we are going. His journey is to the abode of the unfortunate, which is the abode of all those who deny the power and wisdom of Allah and reject the words of all those who were sent by their Lord."

"These are the ones who had disbelieved in their Lord. They will have shackles upon their necks, and they are the companions of the Fire; they will abide in it eternally." *(13: 5)*

"And they say, 'When we disappeared into the earth, shall we indeed be recreated anew?' In fact they deny the meeting with their Lord. Say, 'The angel of death put in charge of you will reclaim you, and then you will be brought back to your Lord.' If you only could see the wrongdoers hang their heads before their Lord: Our Lord, now that we have seen and heard, send us back and we shall do good deeds. (Now) we are convinced." *(32: 10-12)*

As for our journey, O Muslims who have faith in meeting their Lord and believe in His Books and His Messengers, it is to everlasting pleasure, eternal life, noble place and Paradise as wide as the skies and the earth. They will enjoy being close to the Lord of the worlds, the Most Merciful, the

Most Powerful, the Most Just Judge. To Him belong the creation and the command. He holds the benefit and the harm in His hand. He is the First with truth, inevitably Existent, recognised by instinct. The reasons acknowledge Him and all existing things confirm Him. All creatures bear witness on His Oneness and Lordship, and natural disposition attests it. Every move and halt and all that is and will be testify His existence and Ever-Living. It is He who created the heavens and the earth, sent down rain from the sky with which He causes gardens of delight of all kinds to grow, and spread by it all the living creatures on earth.

"Who is it that made the earth a stable place to live? Who made rivers to flow through it? Who set immovable mountains on it and created a barrier between two seas (of the fresh and salt water)? *(27:61)*

He is the one who answers the desperate one when he calls upon Him, and helps the troubled when he calls out, removes the harm and relieves from the distress. It is He who guides His creature in the darkness of land and sea, and sends winds as good tidings before His mercy and restores the earth to life with rain. He is the one who begins the creation then repeats it. He provides all His creatures in the heavens and the earth with their sustenance. He controls hearing, sight and hearts, brings forth the living from the dead and the dead from the living and He governs everything.

"Say, 'Who holds control of everything in His hand? Who protects while there is no protection against Him, if you know?'" *(23:88)*

"It is He who has control over the heavens and earth and has no offspring - no one shares control with Him - and who created all things and made them to an exact measure." *(25:2)*

It is He whose help is sought in every mishap and calamity, well known for generosity and honour. Every voice is hushed for Him, and only a whisper is heard. The heavens and the earth and all creation celebrate His praise. The souls get tranquility in His love, the hearts find peace in His remembrance and the reasons thrive by His knowledge. His help can achieve success and the breeze of His kindness and graciousness revives hearts. Nothing takes place without His order. The one who is lost does not get the way without His guidance. Those who are in need get support from Him. No one is able to understand without His help, and no one can get out of a mishap except by His mercy. Things are taken care of by His protection. Deeds are to start with His name, and are completed by His praise. The desires are attained by His facilitation, and happiness can be achieved only by His obedience. Life depends on His remembrance, love and knowledge. The pleasure of Paradise is not complete without listening to His words and looking at Him. His mercy and knowledge embrace everything and He has covered every living creature by His favour and bounty.

He is the true object of worship, the true Lord and the true King. He is absolutely perfect from every side and pure from all defects and faults whatsoever. The people engaged in His praise cannot fulfil its due though they consume all the time and use all sorts of praise. His praise is above every praise and nothing can match His praise by Him.

He is the Lord in whom the righteous people believe. As for the house they are going to be lodged in is beyond any description. Nobody has any knowledge of its beauty, magnificence, spaciousness, pleasure, splendour and comfort. It has what no eye has seen, no ear has heard of and no thought of it has passed, in any mind. They will have all that their souls desire and eyes delight in. It contains all kinds of the sources of delight and happiness, free from any disgusting and unpleasant matters. It has moving aromatic plants, lofty castles, attractive spouses and tasty fruits. This is the place to which we, O truthful and sincere people, are travelling by the help and support and favour of our Lord.

The journey of those who denied the truth is to the house, which has been prepared for those who disbelieve in Allah and meeting with Him, and reject His Books and Messengers. Allah is not going to put together those who worshipped Allah alone, who strived to achieve His pleasure, exerted in His obedience and worked hard in His way, with those who denied Allah, were active in deeds of His displeasure, continuously disobeyed Him and exerted all their efforts in achieving vain desires. The two groups are not going to be put in one place except for the matters of crossing, as they lived together in this world. The Almighty will bring them together on the Plain of Resurrection and then separate them. His wisdom and perfectness will not allow Him to treat them equally.

On this level you will come to know the life of martyrs. You will notice that they are alive and provided for with their Lord. Their life there is far better and pleasant than this one. Their bodies have disintegrated and their limbs are torn into pieces and their bones decayed. It is not the bodies but the souls. Allah said:
"Do not think of those who have been killed in Allah's way as dead. They are alive with their Lord, well provided for." *(3: 169)*

"Do not say that those who are killed in Allah's cause are dead; they are alive, though you do not realise it." *(2: 154)*

If the martyrs get this life for following the messengers and obeying them then what do you think about the life of the messengers in *Barzakh*? A man has beautifully said:
"Life is slumber and death is waking up; a man who is between these two is just a continuing imagination."

The messengers, martyrs and righteous people's lives, who wake up from the sleep of the world, have more a perfect and complete life. In accordance with the struggle of a man in this world, will be his desire of that world. He will be working and making effort to acquire that life. Allah's help is sought.

10. Life in the Hereafter

The tenth level of life is the one which comes after this existing life and the passing away of its people, and which is everlasting. This is the life upon which the serious people embark and the lucky ones strive for. This is the life that the Books and the Messengers of Allah revealed. It is the one that the unfortunate miss, as described in the Qur'an:

"No indeed! When the earth is pounded to dust, pounded and pounded, when your Lord comes with the angels, row after row, when Hell is that Day brought near – on that Day man will take heed, but what good will that be to him? He will say, 'Would that I had provided for this life to come! On that Day, no one will punish as He punishes, and no one will bind as He binds." *(89: 21-26)*

This is the life about which Allah said:
"This present life is merely an amusement and a diversion; the true life is in the Hereafter, if only they knew." *(29: 64)*

The previous life is like sleep in comparison to this. All that is said about travelling and its stations as well as the conditions of travellers and their internal and external devotion, is only a means to reach it. The Prophet ﷺ described the present life with regard to the next one. He said: "The world in regard to the Hereafter is no more than as one of you puts his finger in the sea, let him see how it returns."

It is also said that the Hereafter took a breath and the world was the result of one breath. The breath of its bounty reached the fortunate people and they are working with this. The breath of its torment reached the wretched ones and they are busy in that.

If the life of the people of faith and good righteous deeds is pleasant in this world, then what will be their life in *Barzakh* be when they are rid of the prison of the world and its constrained place? Furthermore, what will be their life in the abode of everlasting pleasure, which is not going to end? In that they will be honoured to look at the face of their Lord in the morning and evening and listen to His words.

You may ask what is the cause of people being indifferent to that world and not striving for it, and their desire in this vanishing world, which is no more than imagination and slumber? Is it because of their lack of understanding or disbelief in that life? Is it due to the impairment of their reasoning faculty or just preference of that which is seen by eyes over what cannot be seen and known only by faith?

The answer will be that it is due to the complex reasons of all of that. The most powerful cause in this respect is the weakness of faith. Faith is the spirit of the deeds. It encourages good deeds, commanding what is righteous and forbidding what is abhorrent. Its command and prohibition are based on the strength of faith and the obedience of the person is based on it. Allah, the Most High, said:
"How evil are the things your belief commands you to do, if you are really believers! *(2: 93)*

In general, when the faith is strong, the longing to this life will be stronger and its search will be more powerful.

The second cause of people lagging behind in the search of the permanent life is the domination of the negligence on the heart. Negligence is the slumber of the heart. This is the reason you may find many people who seem to be awake asleep in reality. It is the opposite of the condition of the person whose heart is awake while he is asleep. It is because when the life is sound in the heart, it does not fall asleep when the body is asleep. The perfect condition of it was available to our Prophet ﷺ. It could be achieved by anyone whose heart has been endowed with life by Allah Almighty because of his love for Him, and by following the Messenger. It is in accordance with his share of both of these things.

Negligence and wakefulness are in sense, reason and heart. The person who is awake in heart or careless is like the one whose body is awake or careless. As the wakefulness of the sense is of two types, equally in the same way the wakefulness of the heart is of two types.

The first type of the wakefulness of sense makes the person deal with the matters and carry them out with his intelligence, shrewdness and artful means.

The second type makes him turn to his heart and soul and struggle to acquire perfection. He watches the superior and inferior matters and chooses the superior ones. He prefers the better of two good things, leaving aside the less important one, and he indulges in the lighter evil with the fear of falling in the worse one. He adorns himself with noble characters and excellent behaviour. His outward appearance is beautiful and his inward is even more attractive. His secret character is better than his open one. He competes with the people of excellent manners to achieve them, in the same way those greedy of money rush to get it. With this vigilance he becomes ready for two other things:
Firstly, he attains vigilance that pushes him to acquire the permanent invaluable life from the life that has no value. You may ask how it is that he acquires everlasting life from the vanishing one. How could this happen?

My answer is that it is also the result of sleep, or rather death of the heart. Is there any other way to acquire the everlasting life except from this vanishing life? You are trying to kindle your lamp from another lamp, which is about to die out. The second one is going to be very bright and its light will continue, while the first one is doomed to disappear. The person who acquires for his everlasting life from this perishable one moves from a vanishing house to a lasting one. Death separates both. It is a bridge he has to cross to reach the permanent house and a gate through which only he can enter it. They are two lives separated by death. The light of that life is derived from the light of this one and its life is taken from it. A person will have the light in that house in accordance with the light of this world, and his life in that abode will be according to his life in this world.

This light and life which are acquired from the light and life of the world will not die, but rather give light to the person in *Barzakh*, on the Bridge and the plain of the Day of Resurrection. It will accompany him to the everlasting place. The light of the sun will come to an end, but this light will remain. The physical life will end but this life will last. This is one of the two types of the wakefulness of the heart.

The second type of wakefulness is that which produces a life that cannot be described in words. No imagination can reach it and no expression can explain its meaning. It could be pointed out by the life of the lover with his beloved. His heart, soul and life cannot survive without his beloved. His eyes will not get rest, his heart will not be at peace and his soul will not be comfortable, except with his beloved. He needs Him more than he needs his hearing, sight and strength, or rather his life. His life is torment and pain without Him, and he will suffer from grief and worries. His life depends on being close to Him and in His vicinity. The pain of His barrier from him is greater than any other torment. The delight of the heart and soul rests on removal of that barrier. This delight is far greater than the pleasure of eating and drinking and enjoying the company of the beautiful-eyed maidens. In the same way the torment of the barrier is more painful than the torment of Hell. That is why Allah, the Most High, has combined for His devoted servants the two delights when He said:
"Those who did well will have the best reward and more beside." *(10: 26)*

The best reward is Paradise and the 'more' is looking at the noble face of the Lord. He combined two types of torment for His enemies when He said:
"On that Day they will be screened off from their Lord, then they will burn in Hell." *(83: 15-16)*

In general, heedlessness is the sleep of the heart from striving for this life. It is a cover on it. If this cover is removed by remembrance, it is right; otherwise the cover will get thicker until it becomes the cover of idleness and amusement and engagement in what is not useful. Now if he is able to remove it, it will be right, otherwise it will become the cover of disobedience and minor sins, which will put him away from Allah ﷻ. If it is not removed at this stage, it will turn to the cover of major sins, which in turn will cause the wrath and curse of Allah Almighty. After that it will become the cover of innovation in acts in which the person will cause torment for himself without gaining any benefit. If the cover is not removed at this stage, it will become the cover of innovation of belief, which involves telling lies about Allah and His Messenger, and a rejection of the message that the Messenger has brought. If it is not removed, it will become the cover of doubt and rejection, causing damage to the five basic tenets of the faith, which are belief in Allah, His angels, His Books, His messengers and meeting with Him. Because of the thickness and darkness of the cover the person is not able to see the realities of belief. Satan gets hold of him and makes promises and raises false hopes in him. The baser self of him incites him to vain desire and the power of nature gets hold of the belief and imprisons him if they do not destroy him. It becomes in charge of managing his affairs and uses the forces of desires and makes him engaged in customs that are followed by the people. It closes the door of wakefulness and opens the door of negligence. It says to him: 'You should be careful not to be attacked from your side. Take a cover of desire. Do not to let anyone come to me without you. The affairs of this kingdom are in your hands and to the gatekeeper. O gatekeeper of negligence and the chamberlain of the desire, keep to your post. If you leave it the matters of your kingdom will be spoiled and others will get hold of it, and the power of belief will cause us to taste the evil of humiliation and insult. We will never be happy with this city.'"

There is no god except Allah. When these forces attack the heart while the belief has become weak and helpers are very few and the man turns away from the remembrance of the Most Merciful and joins the group of the people of the time, and he in trapped in the long desire that destroys the man and he prefers the existing over the absent, which is promised after this world - only then Allah can give help and one must put his trust in Him.

This is a short and useful chapter about life and its kinds. It is meant to raise the desires to its most honourable and pleasant one. If it finds a heart that has life, it will benefit from it, otherwise it will be like a beautiful virgin who is wed to a blind and handicapped person.

ARABIC ORIGINAL TEXT

Written by Ibn Qayyim al-Jawziyyah

قال صاحب «المنازل»(١): «(باب الحياة)» قال الله تعالى: ﴿أَوَ مَنْ كَانَ مَيْتًا فَأَحْيَيْنَاهُ﴾ [الأنعام/ ١٢٢].

* استشهاده بهذه الآية: في هذا الباب ظاهر جدًا. فإن المراد بها: من كان ميت القلب، بعدم روح العلم والهدى والإيمان. فأحياه الرب تعالى بروح أخرى، غير الروح التي أحيا بها بدنه. وهي روح معرفته وتوحيده، ومحبته وعبادته وحده لا شريك له. إذ لا حياة للروح إلا بذلك. وإلا فهي في جملة الأموات. ولهذا وصف الله تعالى مَنْ عَدَم ذلك بالموت، فقال. ﴿أَوَ مَنْ كَانَ مَيْتًا فَأَحْيَيْنَاهُ﴾ وقال تعالى: ﴿إِنَّكَ لَا تُسْمِعُ الْمَوْتَىٰ ۖ وَلَا تُسْمِعُ الصُّمَّ الدُّعَاءَ﴾ [النمل/ ٨٠]، وسمى وحيه روحًا. لما يحصل به من حياة القلوب والأرواح. فقال تعالى: ﴿وَكَذَٰلِكَ أَوْحَيْنَا إِلَيْكَ رُوحًا مِنْ أَمْرِنَا ۚ مَا كُنْتَ تَدْرِي مَا الْكِتَابُ وَلَا الْإِيمَانُ وَلَٰكِنْ جَعَلْنَاهُ نُورًا نَهْدِي بِهِ مَنْ نَشَاءُ مِنْ عِبَادِنَا﴾ [الشورى/ ٥٢] فأخبر: أنه «روح» تحصل به الحياة، وأنه «نور» تحصل به الإضاءة. وقال تعالى: ﴿يُنَزِّلُ الْمَلَائِكَةَ بِالرُّوحِ مِنْ أَمْرِهِ عَلَىٰ مَنْ يَشَاءُ مِنْ عِبَادِهِ أَنْ أَنْذِرُوا أَنَّهُ لَا إِلَٰهَ إِلَّا أَنَا فَاتَّقُونِ﴾ [النحل/ ٢]، وقال تعالى: ﴿رَفِيعُ الدَّرَجَاتِ ذُو الْعَرْشِ يُلْقِي الرُّوحَ مِنْ أَمْرِهِ عَلَىٰ مَنْ يَشَاءُ مِنْ عِبَادِهِ لِيُنْذِرَ يَوْمَ التَّلَاقِ﴾ [غافر/ ١٥] فالوحي حياة الروح، كما أن الروح حياة البدن. ولهذا من فقد هذه الروح: فقد فقَد الحياة النافعة في الدنيا والآخرة. أما في الدنيا: فحياته حياة البهائم. وله المعيشة الضنك. وأما في الآخرة: فله جهنم، لا يموت فيها ولا يحيا.

● [الحياة الطيبة في الدنيا للعارفين بالله]

وقد جعل الله الحياة الطيبة لأهل معرفته ومحبته وعبادته. فقال تعالى: ﴿مَنْ عَمِلَ صَالِحًا مِنْ ذَكَرٍ أَوْ أُنْثَىٰ وَهُوَ مُؤْمِنٌ فَلَنُحْيِيَنَّهُ حَيَاةً طَيِّبَةً ۖ وَلَنَجْزِيَنَّهُمْ أَجْرَهُمْ بِأَحْسَنِ مَا كَانُوا يَعْمَلُونَ﴾ [النحل/ ٩٧]، وقد فسرت «الحياة الطيبة» بالقناعة والرضى، والرزق الحسن وغير ذلك.

والصواب: أنها حياة القلب ونعيمه، وبهجته وسروره بالإيمان ومعرفة الله، ومحبته، والإنابة إليه، والتوكل عليه. فإنه لا حياة أطيب من حياة صاحبها. ولا نعيم فوق نعيمه، إلا نعيم الجنة، كما كان بعض العارفين يقول: «إنه لَتمرّ بى أوقات أقول فيها: إن كان أهل الجنة في مثل هذا إنهم لفى عيش طيب». وقال غيره: «إنه ليمر بالقلب أوقات يرقُص فيها طرَبًا».

وإذا كانت حياة القلب حياة طيبة تبعتها حياة الجوارح. فإنه ملكها. ولهذا جعل الله المعيشة الضنَك لمن أعرض عن ذكره. وهي عكس الحياة الطيبة.

---

(١) المنازل (ص/ ٤١).

* وهذه الحياة الطيبة تكون فى الدور الثلاث . (أعنى: دار الدنيا، ودار البَرْزخ، ودار القرار) . والمعيشة الضنك أيضًا تكون فى الدور الثلاث. فالأبرار فى النعيم هنا وهنالك . والفجار فى الجحيم هنا وهنالك، قال الله تعالى: ﴿للذين أحسنوا فى هذه الدنيا حسنة ولدار الآخرة خير﴾[النحل/ ٣٠] ، وقال تعالى: ﴿وأن استغفروا ربكم ثم توبوا إليه يمتعكم متاعًا حسنًا إلى أجل مسمى. ويُؤْت كل ذى فَضْلٍ فضله﴾[هود/٣] فذكرَ الله سبحانه وتعالى، ومحبته وطاعته، والإقبالُ عليه: ضامن لأطيب الحياة فى الدنيا والآخرة. والإعراض عنه والغفلة ومعصيته: كفيل بالحياة المنغصة، والمعيشة الضنك فى الدنيا والآخرة.

فصل [تعريف الهروي للحياة]

قال صاحب «المنازل»: «الحياة في هذا الباب: يشار بها إلى ثلاثة أشياء. الحياة الأولى: حياة العلم من موت الجهل، ولها ثلاثة أنفاس: نفس الخوف، ونفس الرجاء، ونفس المحبة»(1).

※ قوله «الحياة في هذا الباب»: يريد: الحياة الخاصة التي يتكلم عليها القوم دون الحياة العامة المشتركة بين الحيوان كله، بل بين الحيوان والنبات. وللحياة مراتب. ونحن نشير إليها:

● [المراتب العامة للحياة]

المرتبة الأولى: (حياة الأرض بالنبات). قال تعالى: ﴿والله أنزل من السماء ماءً. فأحيا به الأرض بعد موتها. إن في ذلك لآيةً لقوم يسمعون﴾ [النحل/ 65]، وقال في الماء: ﴿وأحيينا به بلدةً ميتاً. كذلك الخروج﴾ [ق/ 11] وقال: ﴿وأنزلنا من السماء ماءً طهوراً * لنحيي به بلدةً ميتاً﴾ [الفرقان/ 48، 49] وجعل هذه الحياة دليلاً على الحياة يوم المعاد. وهذه حياة حقيقة في هذه المرتبة، مستعملة في كل لغة، جارية على ألسن الخاصة والعامة. قال الشاعر يمدح عبد المطلب:

بشيبة الحمد أحيا الله بلدتنا   لما فقدنا الحيا، واجلَوَّذ المطر

وهذا أكثر من أن نذكر شواهده.

المرتبة الثانية: (حياة النمو والاغتذاء). وهذه الحياة مشتركة بين النبات والحيوان الذي يعيش بالغذاء. قال الله تعالى: ﴿وجعلنا من الماء كل شيء حيٍّ﴾ [الأنبياء/ 30].

وقد اختلف الفقهاء في الشعور: هل تحلها الحياة؟ على قولين. والصواب: أنها تحلها حياة النمو والغذاء، دون الحس والحركة. ولهذا لا تنجس بالموت. إذ لو أوجب لها فراق النمو والاغتذاء النجاسة: لنجس الزرع والشجر لمفارقته هذه الحياة له. ولهذا كان الجمهور على أن الشعور لا تنجس بالموت(2).

المرتبة الثالثة: (حياة الحيوان المغتذي بقدر زائد على نموه واغتذائه). وهي إحساسه

---

(1) المنازل (ص/ 41).

(2) بهامش مطبوعة المنار ما نصه: وافق الفقهاء على فلسفتهم في علة النجاسة. والصواب. أن النجاسة إنما تحصل بالتعفن والنتن في المركبات ذات الرطوبة التي تتولد فيها الديدان الخفية والظاهرة. وليس ذلك خاصاً بالأجسام ذات الشعور والحركة بالإرادة. فإن قيل: إن ما ذكرته هو القدر الحقيقي الجدير بأن يسمى نجاسة في اللغة. وهم يعنون النجاسة الشرعية. أقول: لا نص في الكتاب والسنة على أن فقد الحس والحركة هو علة النجاسة أو من عللها - الفقي، وانظر في هذه المسألة (التنقيح للذهبي مسألة رقم/ 18).

وحركته. ولهذا يألم بورود الكيفيات المؤلمة عليه، وبتفرق الاتصال، ونحو ذلك. وهذه الحياة فوق حياة النبات. وهذه الحياة تقوى وتضعف في الحيوان الواحد بحسب أحواله. فحياته بعد الولادة: أكمل منها وهو جنين في بطن أمه. وحياته وهو صحيح معافى: أكمل منها وهو سقيم عليل.

فنفس هذه الحياة تتفاوت تفاوتًا عظيمًا في محالها. فحياة الحية أكمل من حياة البعوضة. ومن قال غير هذا فقد كابر الحس والعقل.

المرتبة الرابعة: (حياة الحيوان الذي لا يغتذي بالطعام والشراب). كحياة الملائكة، وحياة الأرواح بعد مفارقتها لأبدانها. فإن حياتها أكمل من حياة الحيوان المغتذي. ولهذا لا يلحقها كلال ولا فتور، ولا نوم ولا إعياء. قال تعالى: ﴿يسبحون الليل والنهار لا يَفْتُرون﴾ [الأنبياء/ ٢٠] وكذلك الأرواح إذا تخلصت من هذه الأبدان، وتجردت: صار لها حياة أخرى أكمل من هذه إن كانت سعيدة. وإن كانت شقية: كانت عاملة ناصبة في العذاب.

المرتبة الخامسة: (الحياة التي أشار إليها المصنف). وهي «حياة العلم من موت الجهل» فإن الجهل موت لأصحابه. كما قيل:

| وأجسامهـم قبـل القبـور قبــورُ | وفي الجهـل ــ قبل الموت ــ موت لأهله |
| فليـس لهـم حتى النشـور نشـورُ | وأرواحهم في وَحْشـة من جسومهــم |

فإن الجاهل ميت القلب والروح، وإن كان حي البدن. فجسده قبر يمشى به على وجه الأرض. قال الله تعالى: ﴿أَوَمَن كان ميتًا فأحييناه. وجعلنا له نورًا يمشى به في الناس. كمن مثله في الظلمات ليس بخارج منها﴾ [الأنعام/ ١٢٢]، وقال تعالى: ﴿إن هو إلا ذكر وقرآن مبين. لينذر من كان حيًا. ويحقّ القول على الكافرين﴾ [يس/ ٦٩، ٧٠] وقال تعالى: ﴿فإنك لا تسمع الموتى ولا تسمع الصم الدعاء﴾ [الروم/ ٥٢]، وقال تعالى: ﴿إن الله يسمع من يشاء. وما أنت بمسمع من في القبور﴾ [فاطر/ ٢٢] وشبههم ــ في موت قلوبهم ــ بأهل القبور. فإنهم قد ماتت أرواحهم. وصارت أجسامهم قبورًا لها. فكما أنه لا يسمع أصحاب القبور، كذلك لا يسمع هؤلاء. وإذا كانت الحياة هي الحس والحركة، وملزومهما. فهذه القلوب لما لم تحس بالعلم والإيمان، ولم تتحرك له: كانت ميتة حقيقة. وليس هذا تشبيهًا لموتها بموت البدن، بل ذلك موت القلب والروح.

وقد ذكر الإمام أحمد في «كتاب الزهد» من كلام لقمان، أنه قال لابنه: «يا بني جالس العلماء، وزاحمهم بركبتيك. فإن الله يحيى القلوب بنور الحكمة، كما يحيى الأرض بوابل القطر». وقال معاذ بن جبل رضي الله عنه: «تعلموا العلم. فإن تعلمه لله خشية، وطلبه عبادة، ومذاكرته تسبيح، والبحث عنه جهاد، وتعليمه لمن لا يعلمه صدقة، وبَذْلُه لأهله

قُربة. لأنه معالم الحلال والحرام، ومنار سُبل أهل الجنة. وهو الأنيس في الوحشة، والصاحب في الغربة، والمحدث في الخلوة، والدليل على السراء والضراء، والسلاح على الأعداء، والزين عند الأخلاء، يرفع الله به أقوامًا، فيجعلهم في الخير قادة، وأئمة تُقتصّ آثارهم، ويُقتدى بأفعالهم، ويُنتهى إلى رأيهم. ترغب الملائكة في خُلَّتهم، وبأجنحتها تمسحهم. يستغفر لهم كل رطب ويابس، وحيتان البحر وهوامُّه، وسباع البر وأنعامه لأن العلم حياة القلوب من الجهل، ومصابيح الأبصار من الظلم، يبلغ العبد بالعلم منازل الأخيار، والدرجات العلى في الدنيا والآخرة. التفكر فيه يعدل الصيام، ومدارسته تعدل القيام. به توصل الأرحام. وبه يعرف الحلال من الحرام. وهو إمام العمل. والعمل تابع له. يلهمه السعداء. ويُحرمه الأشقياء» رواه الطبراني وابن عبد البر وغيرهما. وقد روي مرفوعًا إلى النبي ﷺ. والوقف أصح.

والمقصود: قوله «لأن العلم حياة القلوب من الجهل»: فالقلب ميت. وحياته بالعلم والإيمان.

المرتبة السادسة: (حياة الإرادة والهمة). وضعف الإرادة والطلب من ضعف حياة القلب. وكلما كان القلب أتم حياة، كانت همته أعلى، وإرادته ومحبته أقوى. فإن الإرادة والمحبة تتبع الشعور بالمراد المحبوب، وسلامة القلب من الآفة التي تحول بينه وبين طلبه وإرادته. فضعف الطلب، وفتور الهمة: إما من نقصان الشعور والإحساس، وإما من وجود الآفة المضعفة للحياة. فقوة الشعور، وقوة الإرادة: دليل على قوة الحياة. وضعفهما دليل على ضعفها. وكما أن علو الهمة، وصدق الإرادة، والطلب من كمال الحياة: فهو سبب إلى حصول أكمل الحياة وأطيبها. فإن الحياة الطيبة إنما تنال بالهمة العالية، والمحبة الصادقة، والإرادة الخالصة. فعلى قدر ذلك تكون الحياة الطيبة، وأخسّ الناس حياة أخسهم همة. وأضعفهم محبة وطلبًا، وحياة البهائم خير من حياته. كما قيل:

وَلَيْلُـكَ نَـوْمٌ والـرَّدَى لَـكَ لازمٌ	نهـارك، يـا مغـرور سَهْـوٌ وغفلـة
كذلك في الدنيا تعيش البهائم	وتكـدح فيمـا سـوف تنكـر غِبَّـه
كما غرَّ باللذات ـ في النوم ـ حالم	تُسَـرُّ بمـا يَفْنـى. وتفـرح بالمُنَى

والمقصود: أن حياة القلب بالعلم والإرادة والهمة. والناس إذا شاهدوا ذلك من الرجل. قالوا: هو حيُّ القلب، وحياة القلب بدوام الذكر، وترك الذنوب، كما قال عبدالله ابن المبارك . رحمه الله :

رأيت الذنوب تميت القلوب	وقد يورث الـذل إدمانهـا
وترك الذنوب حياة القلوب	وَخَــيرٌ لنفسـك عصيانها
وهـل أفسـد الدين إلا الملوك، وأحبار سوء ورُهبانها ؟	
وباعوا النفوس، ولم يربحوا	ولم يغلُ في البيع أثمانها
فقد رتّع القـوم فى جيفـة	يبين لـذى اللـب خسرانهـا

وسمعت شيخ الإسلام ابن تيمية - رحمه الله - يقول: من واظب على «يا حي يا قيوم. لا إله إلا أنت» كل يوم - بين سنة الفجر وصلاة الفجر - أربعين مرة. أحيى الله بها قلبه(1).

وكما أن الله سبحانه جعل حياة البدن بالطعام والشراب. فحياة القلب: بدوام الذكر، والإنابة إلى الله، وترك الذنوب، والغفلة الجاثمة على القلب. والتعلق بالرذائل والشهوات المنقطعة عن قريب يضعف هذه الحياة. ولا يزال الضعف يتوالى عليه حتى يموت. وعلامة موته: أنه لا يعرف معروفًا. ولا ينكر منكرًا. كما قال عبد الله بن مسعود - رضى الله عنه -: «أتدرون من ميت القلب، الذى قيل فيه:

ليس من مات فاستراح بميت	إنما الميت ميت الأحيـاء ؟

قالوا: ومن هو؟ قال: «الذى لا يعرف معروفًا ولا ينكر منكرًا».

والرجل: هو الذى يخاف موت قلبه، لا موت بدنه . إذ أكثر هؤلاء الخلق يخافون موت أبدانهم، ولا يبالون بموت قلوبهم. ولا يعرفون من الحياة إلا الحياة الطبيعية، وذلك من موت القلب والروح. فإن هذه الحياة الطبيعية شبيهة بالظل الزائل، والنبات السريع الجفاف، والمنام الذى يخيل كأنه حقيقة. فإذا استيقظ عرف أنه كان خيالاً. كما قال عمر بن الخطاب رضى الله عنه: «لو أن الحياة الدنيا - من أولها إلى آخرها - أوتيها رجل واحد . ثم جاءه الموت: لكان بمنزلة من رأى فى منامه ما يسرُه، ثم استيقظ. فإذا ليس فى يده شىء» وقد قيل: «إن الموت موتان: موت إرادى، وموت طبيعى. فمن أمات نفسه موتًا إراديًا كان موته الطبيعى حياة له» ومعنى هذا: أن الموت الإرادى: هو قمع الشهوات المردية، وإخماد نيرانها المحرقة، وتسكين هوائجها المتلفة، فحينئذ يتفرغ القلب والروح للتفكر فيما فيه كمال

---

(1) انظر مثل هذه الفائدة كتابنا «الحرز الربانى» باب: الحرز الكبير.

العبد، ومعرفته، والاشتغال به. ويرى حينئذ أن إيثار الظل الزائل عن قريب على العيش اللذيذ الدائم: أخسر الخسران. فأما إذا كانت الشهوات وافدة، واللذات مؤثرة، والعوائد غالبة، والطبيعة حاكمة. فالقلب حينئذ: إما أن يكون أسيرًا ذليلًا، أو مهزومًا مُخرَجًا عن وطنه ومستقره الذى لا قرار له إلا فيه، أو قتيلًا ميتًا وما لجرح به إيلام. وأحسن أحواله: أن يكون فى حرب له، يدال له فيها مرة، ويدال عليه مرة. فإذا مات العبد موته الطبيعى: كانت بعده حياة روحه بتلك العلوم النافعة، والأعمال الصالحة، والأحوال الفاضلة التى حصلت له بإماتة نفسه. فتكون حياته هاهنا على حسب موته الإرادى فى هذه الدار.

وهذا موضع لا يفهمه إلا ألبّاء الناس وعقلاؤهم. ولا يعمل بمقتضاه إلا أهل الهمم العلية، والنفوس الزكية الأبية.

المرتبة السابعة – من مراتب الحياة: (حياة الأخلاق، والصفات المحمودة) التى هى حياة راسخة للموصوف بها. فهو لا يتكلف الترقى فى درجات الكمال. ولا يشق عليه. لاقتضاء أخلاقه وصفاته لذلك، بحيث لو فارق ذلك لفارق ما هو من طبيعته وسَجِيَّتِه. فحياة من قد طبع على الحياء والعفة والجود والسخاء، والمروءة والصدق والوفاء ونحوها: أتم من حياة من يقهر نفسه، ويغالب طبعه، حتى يكون كذلك. فإن هذا بمنزلة من تعارضه أسباب الداء وهو يعالجها ويقهرها بأضدادها، وذلك بمنزلة من قد عوفى من ذلك.

وكلما كانت هذه الأخلاق فى صاحبها أكمل كانت حياته أقوى وأتم. ولهذا كان خُلُق «الحياء» مشتقًا من «الحياة» اسمًا وحقيقة. فأكمل الناس حياة: أكملهم حياء. ونقصان حياء المرء من نقصان حياته. فإن الروح إذا ماتت لم تحس بما يؤلمها من القبائح. فلا تستحيى منها. فإذا كانت صحيحة الحياة أحست بذلك، فاستحيت منه. وكذلك سائر الأخلاق الفاضلة، والصفات الممدوحة تابعة لقوة الحياة، وضدها من نقصان الحياة. ولهذا كانت حياة الشجاع أكمل من حياة الجبان، وحياة السخى أكمل من حياة البخيل. وحياة الفطن الذكى أكمل من حياة الفَدْم البليد(١). ولهذا لما كان الأنبياء – صلوات الله وسلامه عليهم – أكمل الناس حياة حتى إن قوة حياتهم تمنع الأرض أن تبلى أجسامهم – كانوا أكمل الناس فى هذه الأخلاق. ثم الأمثل فالأمثل من أتباعهم.

فانظر الآن إلى حياة حَلّاف مهين هَمَّاز مَشَّاء بنميم، مناع للخير معتد أثيم. عُتُلٍّ بعد ذلك زنيم. وحياة جواد شجاع، برٍّ عادل عفيف محسن – تجد الأول ميتًا بالنسبة إلى الثانى. ولله در القائل:

إذا ما عُدَّ من سقط المتاع   وما للمرء خير فى حياة

---

(١) الفدم: الثقيل الفهم العيى، والبليد: ضعيف الذكاء وقليل النشاط.

المرتبة الثامنة – من مراتب الحياة: (حياة الفرح والسرور، وقرة العين بالله). وهذه الحياة إنما تكون بعد الظفر بالمطلوب، الذي تَقَرُّ به عين طالبه. فلا حياة نافعة له بدونه. وحول هذه الحياة يدندن الناس كلهم. وكلهم قد أخطأ طريقها. وسلك طرقًا لا تفضى إليها. بل تقطعه عنها، إلا أقل القليل.

فدار طلب الكل حول هذه الحياة، وحُرِمَها أكثرهم.

وسبب حرمانهم إياها: ضعف العقل والتمييز والبصيرة، وضعف الهمة والإرادة. فإن مادتها بصيرة وقادة، وهمة نقادة. والبصيرة كالبصر تكون عمى وعَوَرًا وعَمَشًا ورمدًا،

وتامة النور والضياء. وهذه الآفات قد تكون لها بالخلقة في الأصل. وقد تحدث فيها بالعوارض الكسبية.

والمقصود: أن هذه المرتبة من مراتب الحياة هي أعلى مراتبها، ولكن كيف يصل إليها مَن عقله مَسبِيٌّ في بلاد الشهوات، وأمله موقوف على اجتناء اللذات، وسيرته جارية على أسوأ العادات، ودينه مستهلك بالمعاصي والمخالفات، وهمته واقفة مع السفليات، وعقيدته غير منلقاة من مشكاة النبوات؟!.

فهو في الشهوات منغمس، وفي الشبهات متنكس، وعن الناصح معرض، وعلى المرشد معترض، وعن السراء نائم، وقلبه في كل واد هائم. فلو أنه تجرد من نفسه. ورغب عن مشاركة أبناء جنسه. وخرج من ضيق الجهل إلى فضاء العلم. ومن سجن الهوى إلى ساحة الهدى، ومن نجاسة النفس، إلى طهارة القدس: لرأى الإلف الذي نشأ بنشأته، وزاد بزيادته؛ وقوى بقوته، وشرف عند نفسه وأبناء جنسه بحصوله، وسد(¹¹) قذى في عين بصيرته، وشجا في حلق إيمانه، ومرضًا متراميًا إلى هلاكه.

فإن قلت: قد أشرت إلى حياة غير معهودة بين أموات الأحياء، فهل يمكنك وصف طريقها، لأصلَ إلى شيء من أذواقها، فقد بان لي أن ما نحن فيه من الحياة حياة بهيمية، ربما زادت علينا فيها البهائم بخلوها عن المنكرات والمنغصات وسلامة العاقبة؟.

قلت: لعمر الله إن اشتياقك إلى هذه الحياة، وطلب علمها ومعرفتها: لدليل على حياتك. وأنك لست من جملة الأموات.

فأول طريقها: أن تعرف الله، وتهتدي إليه طريقًا يوصلك إليه، ويحرق ظلمات الطبع بأشعة البصيرة، فيقوم بقلبه شاهد من شواهد الآخرة. فينجذب إليها بكليته، ويزهد في

---

(١١) كذا في الأصول. والظاهر أن كلمة «وسد» زائدة. فإن المعنى بدونها صحيح. أو محرفة عن كلمة «وجد» – الفقي.

التعلقات الفانية، ويدأب في تصحيح التوبة، والقيام بالمأمورات الظاهرة والباطنة، وترك المنهيات الظاهرة والباطنة، ثم يقوم حارسًا على قلبه، فلا يسامحه بخطرة يكرهها الله، ولا بخطرة فضول لا تنفعه. فيصفو بذلك قلبه عن حديث النفس ووسواسها. فيُفْدى من أسرها. ويصير طليقًا. فحينئذ يخلو قلبه بذكر ربه، ومحبته والإنابة إليه. ويخرج من بين بيوت طبعه ونفسه، إلى فضاء الخلوة بربه وذكره، كما قيل:

وأخرج من بين البيوت، لعلني أحدث عنك النفس في السر خاليًا

فحينئذ يجتمع قلبه وخواطره وحديث نفسه على إرادة ربه، وطلبه والشوق إليه.

فإذا صدق في ذلك رزق محبة الرسول ﷺ، واستولت روحانيته على قلبه. فجعله إمامه ومعلمه، وأستاذه وشيخه وقدوته، كما جعله الله نبيه ورسوله وهاديًا إليه. فيطالع سيرته ومبادئ أمره ﷺ، وكيفية نزول الوحي عليه، ويعرف صفاته وأخلاقه، وآدابه في حركاته وسكونه، ويقظته ومنامه، وعبادته ومعاشرته لأهله وأصحابه، حتى يصير كأنه معه من بعض أصحابه.

فإذا رسخ قلبه في ذلك: فتح عليه بفهم الوحي المنزل عليه من ربه، بحيث لو قرأ السورة شاهد قلبُه ما أنزلت فيه، وما أريد بها. وحظه المختص به منها، من الصفات والأخلاق، والأفعال المذمومة، فيجتهد في التخلص منها كما يجتهد في الشفاء من المرض المخوف. وشاهد حظَّه من الصفات والأفعال الممدوحة. فيجتهد في تكميلها وإتمامها.

فإذا تمكن من ذلك: انفتح في قلبه عين أخرى. يشاهد بها صفات الرب جل جلاله، حتى تصير لقلبه بمنزلة المرئي لعينه. فيشهد علو الرب سبحانه فوق خلقه، واستواءه على عرشه، ونزول الأمر من عنده بتدبير مملكته، وتكليمه بالوحي، وتكليمه لعبده جبريل به، وإرساله إلى من يشاء بما يشاء، وصعود الأمور إليه، وعرضها عليه.

فيشاهد قلبُه ربًا قاهرًا فوق عباده، آمرًا ناهيًا، باعثًا لرسله، منزلاً لكتبه، معبودًا مطاعًا، لا شريك له، ولا مثيل، ولا عدل له. ليس لأحد معه من الأمر شيء، بل الأمر كله له. فيشهد ربه سبحانه قائمًا بالملك والتدبير، فلا حركة ولا سكون، ولا نفع ولا ضر، ولا عطاء ولا منع، ولا قبض ولا بسط إلا بقدرته وتدبيره، فيشهد قيام الكون كله به، وقيامه سبحانه بنفسه. فهو القائم بنفسه، المقيم لكل ما سواه.

فإذا رسخ قلبه في ذلك: شهد الصفة المصححة لجميع صفات الكمال، وهي «الحياة» التي كمالها يستلزم كمال السمع والبصر، والقدرة والإرادة، والكلام، وسائر صفات

الكمال، وصفة «القيومية» الصحيحة المصححة لجميع الأفعال. فالحى القيوم: من له كل صفة كمال. وهو الفعال لما يريد.

فإذا رسخ قلبه فى ذلك: فُتح له مشهد «القرب» و«المعية» فيشهده سبحانه معه، غير غائب عنه، قريبًا غير بعيد، مع كونه فوق سماواته على عرشه، بائنًا من خلقه، قائمًا بالصنع والتدبير، والخلق والأمر، فيحصل له - مع التعظيم والإجلال - الأنس بهذه الصفة. فيأنس به بعد أن كان مستوحشًا. ويقوى به بعد أن كان ضعيفًا. ويفرح به بعد أن كان حزينًا. ويجد بعد أن كان فاقدًا. فحينئذ يجد طعم قوله: «ولا يزال عبدى يتقرب إلىّ بالنوافل حتى أحبه. فإذا أحببته كنت سمعه الذى يسمع به. وبصره الذى يبصر به. ويده التى يبطش بها. ورجله التى يمشى بها. ولئن سألنى لأعطينه. ولئن استعاذنى لأعيذنه»[1].

فأطيب الحياة على الإطلاق: حياة هذا العبد. فإنه محب محبوب، متقرب إلى ربه، وربه قريب منه. قد صار له حبيبه لفرط استيلائه على قلبه، ولهجة بذكره. وعكوف همته على مرضاته، بمنزلة سمعه وبصره ويده ورجله. وهذه آلات إدراكه وعمله وسعيه، فإن سمع سمع بحبيبه، وإن أبصر أبصر به. وإن بطش بطش به. وإن مشى مشى به.

فإن صعب عليك فهم هذا المعنى، وكونُ المحب الكامل المحبة يسمع ويبصر ويبطش ويمشى بمحبوبه، وذاتُه غائبة عنه. فاضرب عنه صفحًا. وخلِّ هذا الشأن لأهله.

خلِّ الهوى لأناسٍ يُعْرَفون بـه   قد كابدوا الحب حتى لانَ أصعبه

فإن السالك إلى ربه لا تزال همته عاكفة على أمرين: استفراغ القلب فى صدق الحب، ويبذل الجهد فى امتثال الأمر. فلا يزال كذلك حتى يبدو على سره شواهد معرفته، وآثار صفاته وأسمائه. ولكن يتوارى عنه ذلك أحيانًا. ويبدو أحيانًا. يبدو من عين الجود ويتوارى بحكم الفترة. والفترات أمر لازم للعبد. فكل عامل له شِرَّة، ولكل شرة فترة. فأعلاها فترة الوحى. وهى للأنبياء، وفترة الحال الخاص للعارفين، وفترة الهمة للمريدين. وفترة العمل للعابدين. وفى هذه الفترات أنواع من الحكمة والرحمة، والتعرفات الإلهية، وتعريف قدر النعمة. وتجديد الشوق إليها، ومحض التواجد إليها وغير ذلك.

ولا تزال تلك الشواهد تتكرر وتتزايد، حتى تستقر، وينصبغ بها قلبه، وتصير الفترة غير قاطعة له. بل تكون نعمة عليه، وراحة له، وترويحًا وتنفيسًا عنه.

فهمة المحب إذا تعلقت روحه بحبيبه، عاكفًا على مزيد محبته، وأسباب قوتها. فهو يعمل على هذا. ثم يترقى منه إلى طلب محبة حبيبه له. فيعمل على حصول ذلك. ولا

---

(1) [صحيح] رواه البخارى برقم (٦٥٠٢) عن أبى هريرة رضى الله عنه.

يعدم الطلب الأول، ولا يفارقه ألبتة. بل يندرج في هذا الطلب الثاني. فتتعلق همته بالأمرين جميعًا، فإنه إنما يحصل له منزلة «كنت سمعه الذي يسمع به، وبصره الذي يبصر به» بهذا الأمر الثاني. وهو كونه محبوبًا لحبيبه. كما قال في الحديث: «فإذا أحببته كنت سمعه وبصره إلخ» فهو يتقرب إلى ربه، حفظًا لمحبته له، واستدعاء لمحبة ربه له.

فحينئذ يَشُدُّ مئزر الجِدِّ في طلب محبة حبيبه له بأنواع التقرب إليه:

فقلبه: للمحبة والإنابة والتوكل، والخوف والرجاء. ولسانه: للذكر وتلاوة كلام حبيبه. وجوارحه: للطاعات. فهو لا يفتر عن التقرب من حبيبه.

وهذا هو السير المفضي إلى هذه الغاية التي لا تنال إلا به. ولا يتوصل إليها إلا من هذا الباب، وهذه الطريق. وحينئذ تجمع له في سيره جميع متفرقات السلوك: من الحضور، والهيبة، والمراقبة، ونفي الخواطر، وتخلية الباطن.

● [مراتب القرب إلى الله]

فإن المحب يشرع – أولاً – فى التقربات بالأعمال الظاهرة. وهى ظاهر التقرب. ثم يترقى من ذلك إلى حال التقرب. وهو الانجذاب إلى حبيبه بكليته بروحه وقلبه، وعقله وبدنه. ثم يترقى من ذلك إلى حال الإحسان. فيعبد الله كأنه يراه. فيتقرب إليه حينئذ من باطنه بأعمال القلوب: من المحبة والإنابة، والتعظيم والإجلال والخشية. فينبعث حينئذ من باطنه الجود ببذل الروح، والجود فى محبة حبيبه بلا تكلف. فيجود بروحه ونفسه، وأنفاسه وإرادته، وأعماله لحبيبه حالاً، لا تكلفًا، فإذا وجد المحب ذلك فقد ظفر بحال التقرب وسره وباطنه. وإن لم يجد ذلك فهو يتقرب بلسانه وبدنه وظاهره فقط، فَلْيَدُمْ على ذلك وليتكلف التقرب بالأذكار والأعمال على الدوام. فعساه أن يحظى بحال القرب.

ووراء هذا «القرب الباطن» أمرٌ آخر أيضًا وهو شىء لا يعبر عنه بأحسن من عبارة أقرب الخلق إلى الله رسول الله ﷺ عن هذا المعنى. حيث يقول حاكيًا عن ربه تبارك وتعالى: «من تقرب منى شبرًا تقربت منه ذراعًا. ومن تقرب منى ذراعًا تقربت منه باعًا. ومن أتانى يمشى أتيته هرولة»[1] فيجد هذا المحب فى باطنه ذوق معنى هذا الحديث ذوقًا حقيقيًا.

فذكر من مراتب القرب ثلاثة. ونبه بها على ما دونها وما فوقها. فذكر تقرب العبد إليه بالبر. وتقرب سبحانه إلى العبد ذراعًا. فإذا ذاق العبد حقيقة هذا التقرب انتقل منه إلى تقرب الذراع. فيجد ذوق تقرب الرب إليه باعًا. فإذا ذاق حلاوة هذا القرب الثانى: أسرع المشى حينئذ إلى ربه. فيذوق حلاوة إتيانه إليه هرولة. وهاهنا منتهى الحديث، منبهًا على أنه إذا هَرْوَلَ عبده إليه كان قرب حبيبه منه فوق هرولة العبد إليه فإما أن يكون قد أمسك عن ذلك لعظيم شاهد الجزاء، أو لأنه يدخل فى الجزاء الذى لم تسمع به أذن، ولم يخطر على قلب بشر. أو إحالةً له على المراتب المتقدمة. فكأنه قيل له: وقس على هذا. فعلى قدر ما تبذل منك متقربًا إلى ربك: يتقرب إليك بأكثر منه. وعلى هذا فلازم هذا التقرب المذكور فى مراتبه. أى من تقرب إلى حبيبه بروحه وجميع قواه، وإرادته وأقواله وأعماله: تقرب الرب منه سبحانه بنفسه فى مقابلة تقرب عبده إليه.

وليس القرب فى هذه المراتب كلها قرب مسافة حسية، ولا مماسة. بل هو قرب حقيقى. والرب تعالى فوق سماواته على عرشه، والعبد فى الأرض.

وهذا الموضع هو سر السلوك، وحقيقة العبودية. وهو معنى الوصول الذى يدندن حوله القوم.

―――――
(١) [صحيح] رواه البخارى برقم (٧٥٣٧) ومسلم فى كتاب (التوبة/٢) عن أبى هريرة رضى الله عنه.

وملاك هذا الأمر: هو قصد التقرب أولاً. ثم التقرب ثانيًا. ثم حال القرب ثالثًا. وهو الانبعاث بالكلية إلى الحبيب.

وحقيقة هذا الانبعاث: أن تفنَى بمراده عن هواك، وبما منه عن حظك. بل يصير ذلك هو مجموع حظك ومرادك، وقد عرفت أن من تقرب إلى حبيبه بشيء من الأشياء جوزى على ذلك بقرب هو أضعافه. وعرفت أن أعلى أنواع التقرب: تقرب العبد بجملته - بظاهره وباطنه، وبوجوده - إلى حبيبه. فمن فعل ذلك فقد تقرب بكله، ولم تبق منه بقية لغير حبيبه. كما قيل:

لا كان من لسواك فيه بقية   يجد السبيل بها إليه العُذَّل

وإذا كان المتقرب إليه بالأعمال يعطى أضعاف ما تقرب به. فما الظن بمن أُعطى حال التقرب وذوقه ووجده؟ فما الظن بمن تقرب إليه بروحه، وجميع إرادته وهمته، وأقواله وأعماله؟.

● [الجزاء من جنس العمل]

وعلى هذا فكما جاد لحبيبه بنفسه، فإنه أهل أن يُجاد عليه، بأن يكون ربه سبحانه هو حظه ونصيبه، عوضًا عن كل شيء، جزاءً وفاقًا. فإن الجزاء من جنس العمل. وشواهد هذا كثيرة:

منها: قوله تعالى: ﴿ومن يتق الله يجعل له مخرجًا. ويرزقه من حيث لا يحتسب. ومن يتوكل على الله فهو حسبه﴾ [الطلاق/ ٢، ٣]، ففرق بين الجزائين كما ترى. وجعل جزاء المتوكل عليه كونه سبحانه حسبه وكافيه.

ومنها: أن الشهيد لما بذل حياته لله أعاضه الله سبحانه حياة أكمل منها عنده في محل قربه وكرامته.

ومنها: أن من بذل لله شيئًا أعاضه الله خيرًا منه.

ومنها: قوله تعالى: ﴿فاذكروني أذكركم واشكروا لي ولا تكفرون﴾ [البقرة/ ١٥٢].

ومنها: قوله في الحديث القدسي: "من ذكرني في نفسه ذكرته في نفسي، ومن ذكرني في ملإ ذكرته في ملإ خير منه"(١).

ومنها: قوله: "من تقرب مني شبرًا تقربت منه ذراعًا" الحديث(٢).

فالعبد لا يزال رابحًا على ربه أفضل مما قدَّم له. وهذا المتقرب، بقلبه وروحه وعمله: يفتح عليه ربه بحياة لا تشبه ما الناس فيه من أنواع الحياة، بل حياة من ليس كذلك بالنسبة إلى حياته: كحياة الجنين في بطن أمه بالنسبة إلى حياة أهل الدنيا ولذتهم فيها. بل أعظم من ذلك.

فهذا نموذج من بيان شرف هذه الحياة وفضلها. وإن كان علم هذا يوجب لصاحبه حياة طيبة. فكيف إن انصبغ القلب به، وصار حالاً ملازمًا لذاته؟ فالله المستعان.

فهذه الحياة: هي حياة الدنيا ونعيمها في الحقيقة. فمن فقدها ففقده لحياته الطبيعية أولى به.

هذي حياة الفتى. فإن فُقدت   ففقده للحياة اليـــق بـــه

---

(١) [صحيح] رواه أحمد (٢/ ٣٥٤، ٤٠٥) بإسناد صحيح.
(١) [صحيح] تقدم قريبًا.

فلا عيش إلا عيش المحبين، الذين قرَّت أعينهم بحبيبهم، وسكنت نفوسهم إليه، واطمأنت قلوبهم به، واستأنسوا بقربه، وتنعموا بحبه. ففي القلب فاقة لا يَسُدُّها إلا محبة الله، والإقبال عليه، والإنابة إليه، ولا يَلُمُّ شَعَثَهُ بغير ذلك ألبتة. ومن لم يظفر بذلك: فحياته كلها هموم وغموم، وآلام وحسرات. فإنه إن كان ذا همة عالية تقطعت نفسه على الدنيا حسرات. فإن همته لا ترضى فيها بالدون وإن كان مَهينًا خسيسًا فعيشه كعيش أخس الحيوانات. فلا تقر العيون إلا بمحبة الحبيب الأول.

ما الحـب إلا للحبيــب الأول   نَقِّل فؤادك حيث شئتَ من الهوى

وحَنينه أبــدًا لأول منــزل   كـم منزل في الأرض يألَفُه الفتى

المرتبة التاسعة من مراتب الحياة: (حياة الأرواح بعد مفارقتها الأبدان) وخلاصها من هذا السجن وضيقه. فإن من وراءه فضاء وروحًا وريحانًا وراحة. نسبة هذه الدار إليه. كنسبة بطن الأم إلى هذه الدار، أو أدنى من ذلك.

قال بعض العارفين: لتكُنْ مبادرتُك إلى الخروج من الدنيا كمبادرتك إلى الخروج من السجن الضيق إلى أحبتك، والاجتماع بهم في البساتين المونقة. قال الله تعالى في هذه الحياة ﴿فأما إن كان من المقربين ٭ فروح وريحان وجنة نعيم﴾ [الواقعة/ ٨٨، ٨٩].

ويكفي في طيب هذه الحياة: مرافقة الرفيق الأعلى، ومفارقة الرفيق المؤذي المنكد، الذي تنغص رؤيته ومشاهدته الحياة، فضلًا عن مخالطته وعِشْرَته، إلى الرفيق الأعلى الذين أنعم الله عليهم من النبيين والصديقين والشهداء والصالحين وحسن أولئك رفيقًا، في جوار الرب الرحمن الرحيم.

في الموت ألفُ فضيلــة لا تعــرف   قد قلت، إذ مدحوا الحياة فأسرفوا:

وفراق كــل معاشــر لا ينصـف   منها : أمــان لقــائــه بلقــائــه

ولو لم يكن في الموت من الخير إلا أنه باب الدخول إلى هذه الحياة، وجسر يُعْبَر منه إليها: لكفى به تحفة للمؤمن.

أبَرُّ بنــا مـن كــل بَــرٍّ والطـف   جزى الله عنا الموت خيرًا. فإنــه

ويُدْني إلى الدار التي هي أشرف   يُعَجِّل تخليص النفوس من الأذى

فالاجتهاد في هذا العمر القصير، والمدة القليلة، والسعي والكدح، وتحمل الأثقال، والتعب والمشقة: إنما هو لهذه الحياة. والعلوم والأعمال: وسيلة إليها. وهي يَقَظَة. وما قبلها من الحياة نوم. وهي عين، وما قبلها أثر. وهي حياة جامعة بين فقد المكروه،

وحصول المحبوب فى مقام الأنس، وحضرة القدس، حيث لا يتعذر مطلوب، ولا يفقد محبوب. حيث الطمأنينة والراحة، والبهجة والسرور. حيث لا عبارة للعبد عن حقيقة كنهها. لأنها فى بلد لا عهد لنا به. ولا إلف بيننا وبين ساكنه. فالنفس - لإلفها لهذا السجن الضيق النكد زمانًا طويلًا - تكره الانتقال منه إلى ذلك البلد. وتستوحش إذا استشعرت مفارقته.

وحصول العلم بهذه الحياة: إنما وصل إلينا بخبر إلهى، على يد أكمل الخلق وأعلمهم وأنصحهم ﷺ. فقامت شواهدها فى قلوب أهل الإيمان. حتى صارت لهم بمنزلة العيان. ففرت نفوسهم من هذا الظل الزائل، والخيال المضمحل، والعيش الفانى المشوب بالتنغيص وأنواع الغصص، رغبة فى هذه الحياة، وشوقًا إلى ذلك الملكوت، ووجدًا بهذا السرور، وطربًا على هذا الحد، واشتياقًا لهذا النسيم، الوارد من محل النعيم المقيم.

ولعمر الله إن من سافر إلى بلد العدل والخصب، والأمن والسرور: صبَّر فى طريقه على كل مشقة، وإعوازٍ وجدب، وفارق المتخلفين أحوج ما كان إليهم، وأجاب المنادى إذا نادى به: حى على الفلاح. ويبذل نفسه فى الوصول بَذْل المحب بالرضى والسماح، وواصل السير بالغدوّ والرواح. فحمد عند الوصول مَسْراه، وإنما يحمد المسافر السُّرَى عند الصباح.

عند الصباح يحمد القوم السُّرَى   وفى الممات يحمد القوم اللقا

وما هذا - والله - بالصعب ولا بالشديد، مع هذا العمر القصير، الذى هو بالنسبة إلى تلك الدار كساعة من نهار ﴿كَأَنَّهُمْ يَوْمَ يَرَوْنَ مَا يُوعَدُونَ لَمْ يَلْبَثُوا إِلَّا سَاعَةً مِنْ نَهَارٍ﴾ [الأحقاف/٣٥]، ﴿وَيَوْمَ يَحْشُرُهُمْ كَأَنْ لَمْ يَلْبَثُوا إِلَّا سَاعَةً مِنَ النَّهَارِ يَتَعَارَفُونَ بَيْنَهُمْ﴾ [يونس/٤٥]، ﴿كَأَنَّهُمْ يَوْمَ يَرَوْنَهَا لَمْ يَلْبَثُوا إِلَّا عَشِيَّةً أَوْ ضُحَاهَا﴾ [النازعات/٤٦] ﴿وَيَوْمَ تَقُومُ السَّاعَةُ يُقْسِمُ الْمُجْرِمُونَ مَا لَبِثُوا غَيْرَ سَاعَةٍ﴾ [الروم/٥٥] ﴿قَالَ كَمْ لَبِثْتُمْ فِي الْأَرْضِ عَدَدَ سِنِينَ * قَالُوا لَبِثْنَا يَوْمًا أَوْ بَعْضَ يَوْمٍ فَاسْأَلِ الْعَادِّينَ * قَالَ إِنْ لَبِثْتُمْ إِلَّا قَلِيلًا لَوْ أَنَّكُمْ كُنْتُمْ تَعْلَمُونَ﴾ [المؤمنون/١١٢ - ١١٤] فلو أن أحدنا يجرّ على وجهه - يتقى به الشوك والحجارة - إلى هذه الحياة: لم يكن ذلك كثيرًا ولا غبنًا فى جنب ما يُوفّاه.

فواحسرتاه على بصيرة شاهدت هاتين الحياتين على ما هما عليه، وعلى همة تؤثر الأدنى على الأعلى. وما ذاك إلا بتوفيق مَنْ أزمَّةُ الأمور بيديه. ومنه ابتداء كل شىء وانتهاؤه إليه، أقعدَ نفوس من غلبت عليهم الشقاوة عن السفر إلى هذه الدار، وجذب قلوب من سبقت لهم منه الحسنى. وأقامهم فى الطريق، وسهَّل عليهم ركوب الأخطار. فأضاع أولئك مراحل أعمارهم مع المتخلفين وقطع هؤلاء مراحل أعمارهم مع السائرين.

وعُقدت الغَبَرة وثار العَجاج(١)، فتوارى عنه السائرون والمتخلفون. وسينجلي عن قريب. فيفوز العاملون. ويخسر المبطلون.

✽ ومن طيب هذه الحياة ولذتها: قال النبي ﷺ: «ما من نفس تموت – لها عند الله خير – يسرها أن ترجع إلى الدنيا، وأن لها الدنيا وما فيها، إلا الشهيد. فإنه يتمنى الرجوع إلى الدنيا. لما يرى من كرامة الله له»(٢) يعني ليقتل فيه مرة أخرى.

وسمع بعض العارفين منشدًا ينشد:

إنـما العيــش فــى بهيمــية اللــ	ـذة، وهــو مــا يقولــه الفلسفــى
حكم كــأس المنون: أن يتساوى	فى حساهــا البليــد والألمعــى
ويصير الغبــىُّ تحــت ثــرى الأر	ض، كما صار تحتها اللوذعــى
فَسَلِ الأرضَ عنهما إن أزالَ الشــ	ــكَّ والشبهــةَ السـؤالُ الجلــى

فقال: قاتله الله: ما أشد معاندته للدين والعقل! هذا نفَس عدو الفطرة، والشريعة، والعقل والإيمان والحكمة. يا مسكين: أمن أجل أن الموت تساوَى فيه الصالح والطالح، والعالم والجاهل، وصاروا جميعًا تحت أطباق الثرى: أيجب أن يتساووا فى العاقبة؟

أما تساوَى قوم سافروا من بلد إلى بلد فى الطريق؟ فلما بلغوا القصد نزل كل واحد فى مكان كان مُعدًا له، وتُلُقِّى بغير ما تُلُقِّى به رفيقة فى الطريق؟ أما لكل قوم دار فأُجلس كل واحد منهم حيث يليق به؟ وقوبل هذا بشيء، وهذا بضده، أما قدم على الملك من جاءه بما يحبه. فأكرمه عليه، ومن جاءه بما يسخطه، فعاقبه عليه؟ أما قدم ركب المدينة. فنزل بعضهم فى قصورها وبساتينها وأماكنها الفاضلة. ونزل قوم على قوارع الطريق بين الكلاب؟ أما قدم اثنان من بطن الأم الواحدة. فصار هذا إلى المُلْك، وهذا إلى الأسر والعناء؟.

وقولك «سَلِ الأرض عنهما» أما إنا قد سألناها، فأخبرتنا: أنها قد ضمت أجسادهم وجثثهم وأوصالهم، لا كفرهم وإيمانهم، ولا أنسابهم وأحسابهم، ولا حلمهم وسفههم، ولا طاعتهم ومعصيتهم، ولا يقينهم وشكهم، ولا توحيدهم وشركهم، ولا جورهم وعدلهم، ولا علمهم وجهلهم، فأخبرتنا عن هذه الجثث البالية والأبدان المتلاشية، والأوصال المتمزقة، وقالت: هذا خبر ما عندى.

وأما خبر تلك الأرواح، وما صارت إليه: فسلوا عنها كتب رب العالمين، ورسله الصادقين، وخلفاءهم الوارثين. سلوا القرآن، فعنده الخبر اليقين. وسلوا من جاء به، فهو

---

(١) العَجاج: الغبار.
(١) [صحيح] رواه البخارى برقم (٢٨١٧) ومسلم (فى الجهاد/ ١٠٩) عن أنس رضى الله عنه.

بذلك أعرف العارفين. وسلوا العلم والإيمان، فهما الشاهدان المقبولان. وسلوا العقول والفطر، فعندها حقيقة الخبر ﴿أم حسب الذين اجترحوا السيئات أن نجعلهم كالذين آمنوا وعملوا الصالحات سواءً محياهم ومماتهم ساءَ ما يحكمون﴾ [الجاثية/ ٢١]، تعالى الله - أحكم الحاكمين - عن هذا الظن والحسبان. الذى لا يليق إلا بأجهل الجاهلين.

ثم قال: الناظر فى هذا الباب رجلان: رجل ينظر إلى الأشياء، ورجل ينظر فى الأشياء. فالأول: يحار فيها. فإن صورها وأشكالها وتخاطيطها تستفرغ ذهنه وحسه، وتبدد فكره وقلبه. فنظره إليها بعين حسهِ، لا يفيده منها ثمرة الاعتبار، ولا زُبدة الاختبار؛ لأنه لما فقد الاعتبار أولاً، فإنه فقد الاختيار ثانيًا.

وأما الناظر فى الأشياء: فإن نظره يبعثه على العبور من صورها إلى حقائقها والمراد بها. وما اقتضى وجودها من الحكمة البالغة، والعلم التام. فيفيده هذا النظر تمييز مراتبها، ومعرفة نافعها من ضارها، وصحيحها من سقيمها، وباقيها من فانيها، وقشرها من لُبِّها. ويميز بين الوسيلة والغاية، وبين وسيلة الشيء ووسيلة ضده. فيعرف حينئذ أن الدنيا قشر والآخرة لُبّ، وأن الدنيا محل الزرع، والآخرة وقت الحصاد. وأن الدنيا معبر وممر، والآخرة دار مستقر.

وإذا عرف أن الدنيا طريق وممر: كان حَرِيًّا بتهيئة الزاد لقراره، ويعلم حينئذ أنه لم ينشأ فى هذه الدار للاستيطان والخلود. ولكن للجواز إلى مكان آخر، هو المنزل والمتبوأ. وأن الإنسان دُعى إلى ذلك بكل شريعة، وعلى لسان كل نبى، وبكل إشارة ودليل. ونُصِب له على ذلك علم، وضرب لأجله كل مثل. ونبه عليه بنشأته الأولى ومبادئه، وسائر أحواله، وأحوال طعامه وشرابه، وأرضه وسمائه. بحيث أزيلت عنه الشبهة، وأوضحت له المحجة، وأقيمت عليه الحجة. وأعذر إليه غاية الإعذار، وأهل أتم الإمهال. فاستبان لذى العقل الصحيح والفطرة السليمة: أن الظعن(١) عن هذا المكان ضرورى، والانتقال عنه حق لا مِرية فيه. وأن له محلاً آخر. له قد أُنشِئ. ولأجله قد خلق. وله هُيِّئ. فمصيره إليه. وقدومه بلا ريب عليه. وأن داره هذه: منزل عبور، لا منزل قرار.

وبالجملة: من نظر فى الموجودات، ولم يقنع بمجرد النظر إليها وحدها: وجدها دالة على أن وراء هذه الحياة حياة أخرى أكمل منها. وأن هذه الحياة بالنسبة إليها كالمنام بالنسبة إلى اليقظة. وكالظل بالنسبة إلى الشخص، وسمعها كلها تنادى بما نادى به ربها وخالقها وفاطرها ﴿يا أيها الناس إن وعد الله حق فلا تغرنكم الحياة الدنيا ولا يغرنكم بالله الغرور﴾ [فاطر/٥]، وتنادى بلسان الحال؛ بما نادى به ربها بصريح المقال: ﴿واضرب لهم مثل الحياة الدنيا كماء أنزلناه من السماء فاختلط به نبات الأرض فأصبح هشيمًا تذروه الرياح. وكان الله على كل شىء مقتدرًا﴾ [الكهف/ ٤٥]، وقال تعالى: ﴿إنما مثل الحياة الدنيا كماء أنزلناه

---

(١) الظعن: السير والارتحال.

من السماء فاختلط به نبات الأرض مما يأكل الناس والأنعام حتى إذا أخذت الأرض زخرُفها وازّينت وظن أهلها أنهم قادرون عليها أتاها أمرنا ليلاً أو نهاراً فجعلناها حصيداً كأن لم تَغْنَ بالأمس كذلك نفصل الآيات لقوم يتفكرون﴾ [يونس/ ٢٤]، وقال تعالى: ﴿اعلموا أنما الحياة الدنيا لعب ولهو وزينة وتفاخر بينكم وتكاثر فى الأموال والأولاد كمثل غيث أعجب الكفار نباته ثم يهيج فتراه مصفراً ثم يكون حُطاماً وفى الآخرة عذاب شديد ومغفرة من الله ورضوان وما الحياة الدنيا إلا متاع الغرور﴾ [الحديد/ ٢٠]، ثم ندبهم إلى المسابقة إلى الدار الآخرة الباقية التى لا زوال لها. فقال: ﴿سابقوا إلى مغفرة من ربكم وجنةٍ عرضها كعرض السماء والأرض أعدت للذين آمنوا بالله ورسله ذلك فضل الله يؤتيه من يشاء والله ذو الفضل العظيم﴾ [الحديد/ ٢١].

وسمع بعض العارفين منشداً ينشد عن بعض الزنادقة عند موته – وهو محمد بن زكريا الرازى المتطبب:

لعمرى ما أدرى – وقد أذن البِلَى   بعاجل ترحالى – إلى أين ترحالى؟

وأين محل الروح بعد خروجه   عن الهيكل المنحل والجسد البالى؟

فقال: وما علينا من جهله. إذا لم يدر أين ترحاله؟ ولكنا ندرى إلى أين ترحالنا وترحاله. أما ترحاله: فإلى دار الأشقياء، ومحل المنكرين لقدرة الله وحكمته، والمكذبين بما اتفقت عليه كلمة المرسلين عن ربهم: ﴿أولئك الذين كفروا بربهم وأولئك الأغلال فى أعناقهم وأولئك أصحاب النار هم فيها خالدون﴾ [الرعد/ ٥]، ﴿وقالوا أئذا ضللنا فى الأرض أئنا لفى خلق جديد بل هم بلقاء ربهم كافرون * قل يتوفاكم ملك الموت الذى وُكِّل بكم ثم إلى ربكم ترجعون * ولو ترى إذ المجرمون ناكسوا رءوسهم عند ربهم ربنا أبصرنا وسمعنا فارجعنا نعمل صالحاً إنا موقنون﴾ [السجدة/ ١٠ - ١٢].

وأما ترحالنا، أيها المسلمون، المصدقون بلقاء ربهم، وكتبه ورسله: فإلى نعيم دائم، وخلود متصل، ومقام كريم، وجنة عرضها السماوات والأرض فى جوار رب العالمين، وأرحم الراحمين، وأقدر القادرين، وأحكم الحاكمين، الذى له الخلق والأمر، وبيده النفع والضر، الأول بالحق، الموجود بالضرورة، المعروف بالفطرة، الذى أقرت به العقول، ودلت عليه كل الموجودات، وشهدت بوحدانيته وربوبيته جميع المخلوقات، وأقرت بها الفطرة.

المشهود وجوده وقيوميته بكل حركة وسكون، بكل ما كان وما هو كائن وما سيكون. الذى خلق السماوات والأرض وأنزل من السماء ماء فأنبتنا به حدائق ذات بهجة من أنواع النباتات،، وبث به فى الأرض جميع الحيوانات ﴿أمن جعل الأرض قراراً. وجعل خلالها أنهاراً وجعل لها رواسى وجعل بين البحرين حاجزاً﴾ [النمل/ ٦١] الذى يجيب المضطر إذا دعاه، ويغيث الملهوف إذا ناداه. ويكشف السوء ويفرج الكربات. ويقيل العثرات. الذى

يهدى خلقه فى ظلمات البر والبحر، ويرسل الرياح بُشرًا بين يدى رحمته. فيحيى الأرض بوابل القطر. الذى يبدأ الخلق ثم يعيده. ويرزق من فى السماوات والأرض من خلقه وعبيده. الذى يملك السمع والأبصار والأفئدة. ويخرج الحى من الميت. ويخرج الميت من الحى، ويدبر الأمر الذى ﴿بيده ملكوت كل شىء وهو يجير ولا يجار عليه﴾ [المؤمنون/ ٨٨] ﴿الذى له ملك السماوات والأرض ولم يتخذ ولدًا ولم يكن له شريك فى الملك. وخلق كل شىء فقدره تقديرًا﴾ [الفرقان/ ٢] المستعان به على كل نائبة وفادحة، والمعهود منه كل بر وكرامة. الذى عنت له الوجوه، وخشعت له الأصوات، وسبَّحت بحمده الأرض والسماوات، وجميع الموجودات، الذى لا تسكن الأرواح إلا بحبه، ولا تطمئن القلوب إلا بذكره، ولا تزكو العقول إلا بمعرفته، ولا يُدرك النجاح إلا بتوفيقه، ولا تحيا القلوب إلا بنسيم لطفه وقربه، ولا يقع أمر إلا بإذنه، ولا يهتدى ضال إلا بهدايته، ولا يستقيم ذو أود إلا بتقويمه، ولا يفهم أحد إلا بتفهيمه. ولا يُتخلص من مكروه إلا برحمته، ولا يُحفظُ شىء إلا بكلاءته، ولا يُفتتح أمر إلا باسمه، ولا يتم إلا بحمده، ولا يدرك مأمول إلا بتيسيره، ولا تنال سعادة إلا بطاعته، ولا حياة إلا بذكره ومحبته ومعرفته، ولا طابت الجنة إلا بسماع خطابه ورؤيته. الذى وسع كل شىء رحمة وعلمًا، وأوسع كل مخلوق فضلاً وبرًا.

فهو الإله الحق. والرب الحق. والملك الحق. والمنفرد بالكمال المطلق من كل الوجوه. المبرأ عن النقائص والعيوب من كل الوجوه. لا يبلغ المثنون – وإن استوعبوا جميع الأوقات بكل أنواع الثناء – ثناء عليه، بل ثناؤه أعظم من ذلك. فهو كما أثنى على نفسه. هذا الجار.

وأما الدار: فلا تعلم نفس حسنها وبهاءها، وسعتها ونعيمها. وبهجتها وروحها وراحتها. فيها ما لا عين رأت، ولا أذن سمعت. ولا خطر على قلب بشر. فيها ما تشتهى الأنفس، وتلذُّ الأعين. فهى الجامعة لجميع أنواع الأفراح والمسرات، الخالية من جميع المنكدات والمنغصات، ريحانة تهتز، وقصر مشيد، وزوجة حسناء، وفاكهة نضيجة.

فترحالنا أيها – الصادقون المصدقون – إلى هذه الدار بإذن ربنا وتوفيقه وإحسانه.

وترحال الكاذبين المكذبين إلى الدار التى أعدت لمن كفر بالله ولقائه، وكتبه ورسله.

ولن يجمع الله بين الموحدين له – الطالبين لمرضاته، الساعين فى طاعته، الدائبين فى خدمته، المجاهدين فى سبيله – وبين الملحدين، الساعين فى مساخطه، الدائبين فى معصيته، المستفرغين جهدهم فى أهوائهم وشهواتهم: فى دار واحدة، إلا على سبيل الجواز والعبور. كما جمع بينهما فى هذه الدنيا. ويجمع بينهم فى موقف القيامة، فحاشاه من هذا الظن السىء الذى لا يليق بكماله وحكمته.

فصل [حياة الشهداء]

وفى هذه المرتبة تعلم حياة الشهداء، وأنهم عند ربهم يرزقون، وأنها أكمل من حياتهم فى هذه الدنيا، وأتم وأطيب، وإن كانت أجسادهم متلاشية، ولحومهم متمزقة، وأوصالهم متفرقة، وعظامهم نخرة، فليس العمل على الطَّلَلِ، إنما الشأن فى الساكن. قال الله تعالى: ﴿ولا تحسبن الذين قتلوا فى سبيل الله أمواتًا بل أحياء عند ربهم يرزقون﴾ [آل عمران/ ١٦٩]، وقال تعالى: ﴿ولا تقولوا لمن يقتل فى سبيل الله أموات بل أحياء ولكن لا تشعرون﴾ [البقرة/ ١٥٤]، وإذا كان الشهداء إنما نالوا هذه الحياة بمتابعة الرسل وعلى أيديهم، فما الظن بحياة الرسل فى البرزخ؟ ولقد أحسن القائل ما شاء:

فالعيش نوم. والمنية يقظة   والمرء بينهما خيال سارى

فللرسل والشهداء والصديقين من هذه الحياة – التى هى يقظة من نوم الدنيا – أكملها وأتمها. وعلى قدر حياة العبد فى هذا العالم يكون شوقه إلى هذه الحياة، وسعيه وحرصه على الظفر بها. والله المستعان.

المرتبة العاشرة من مراتب الحياة: (الحياة الدائمة الباقية بعد طَىِّ هذا العالم. وذهاب الدنيا وأهلها فى دار الحيوان).

وهى الحياة التى شمر إليها المشمرون. وسابق إليها المتسابقون. ونافس فيها المتنافسون. وهى التى أجرينا الكلام إليها. ونادت الكتب السماوية ورسل الله جميعهم عليها. وهى التى يقول من فاته الاستعداد لها ﴿إذا دُكّت الأرض دكًّا دكًّا * وجاء ربك والملك صفًّا صفًّا * وجىء يومئذ بجهنم يومئذ يتذكر الإنسان وأنى له الذكرى * يقول يا ليتنى قدمت لحياتى * فيومئذ لا يعذّبُ عذابه أحد * ولا يُوثق وثاقه أحد﴾ [الفجر/ ٢١ – ٢٦]، وهى التى قال الله عز وجل فيها: ﴿وما هذه الحياة الدنيا إلا لهو ولعب وإن الدار الآخرة لهى الحيوان لو كانوا يعلمون﴾ [العنكبوت/ ٦٤].

والحياة المتقدمة كالنوم بالنسبة إليها، وكل ما تقدم – من وصف السير ومنازله، وأحوال السائرين، وعبوديتهم الظاهرة والباطنة – فوسيلة إلى هذه الحياة. وإنما الحياة الدنيا، بالنسبة إليها، كما قال النبى ﷺ: «ما الدنيا فى الآخرة إلا كما يُدخل أحدُكم إصبعه فى اليَمِّ فلينظر بم ترجع؟»(١).

وكما قيل: تنفست الآخرة. فكانت الدنيا نفسًا من أنفاسها. فأصاب أهل السعادة نَفَس نعيمها. فهم على هذا النفس يعملون. وأصاب أهل الشقاوة نفس عذابها. فهم على ذلك النفس يعملون.

---

(١) [صحيح] رواه الترمذى برقم (٢٣٢٣) عن المستورد رضى الله عنه وقال: حديث حسن صحيح.

وإذا كانت حياة أهل الإيمان والعمل الصالح في هذه الدار حياة طيبة. فما الظن بحياتهم في البرزخ، وقد تخلصوا من سجن الدنيا وضيقها؟ فما الظن بحياتهم في دار النعيم المقيم الذي لا يزول. وهم يرون وجه ربهم تبارك وتعالى بُكرةً وعشيًّا ويسمعون خطابه؟

● [أسباب غفلة النفس وتخلفها عن طلب هذه الحياة]

فإن قلت: ما سبب تخلف النفس عن طلب هذه الحياة التي لا خَطَرَ لها، وما الذي زَهَّدَها فيها؟ وما سبب رغبتها في الحياة الفانية المضمحلة، التي هي كالخيال والمنام؟ أفسادٌ في تصورها وشعورها؟ أم تكذيب بتلك الحياة؟ أم آفة في العقل، وعمى هناك؟ أم إيثار حاضر المشهود بالعيان على الغائب المعلوم بالإيمان؟

قيل: بل ذلك لمجموع أمور مركبة من ذلك كله.

وأقوى الأسباب في ذلك:

[أولاً]: (ضعف الإيمان). فإن الإيمان هو روح الأعمال. وهو الباعث عليها، والآمر بأحسنها، والناهي عن أقبحها. وعلى قدر قوة الإيمان يكون أمره ونهيه لصاحبه، وائتمار صاحبه وانتهاؤه. قال الله تعالى: ﴿قل بئسما يأمركم به إيمانكم إن كنتم مؤمنين﴾ [البقرة/ ٩٣].

وبالجملة: فإذا قوي الإيمان قوي الشوق إلى هذه الحياة. واشتد طلب صاحبه لها.

السبب الثاني: (جثوم الغفلة على القلب). فإن الغفلة نوم القلب. ولهذا تجد كثيرًا من الأيقاظ في الحس نيامًا في الواقع. فتحسبهم أيقاظًا وهم رقود، ضد حال من يكون يقظان القلب وهو نائم. فإن القلب إذا قويت فيه الحياة لا ينام إذا نام البدن. وكمال هذه الحياة كان لنبينا ﷺ. ولمن أحيا الله قلبه بمحبته واتباع رسالته على بصيرة من ذلك بحسب نصيبه منهما.

فالغفلة واليقظة يكونان في الحس والعقل والقلب، فمستيقظ القلب وغافله كمستيقظ البدن ونائمه. وكما أن يقظة الحس على نوعين. فكذلك يقظة القلب على نوعين:

● [أنواع اليقظة من الغفلة]

فالنوع الأول من يقظة الحس: أن صاحبها ينفذ فى الأمور الحسية. ويتوغل فيها بكسبه وفطانته، واحتياله وحسن تأتيه.

والنوع الثانى: أن يُقبِل على نفسه وقلبه وذاته. فيعتنى بتحصيل كماله. فيلحظ عوالى الأمور وسفسافها. فيؤثر الأعلى على الأدنى. ويقدم خير الخيرين بتفويت أدناهما ويرتكب أخف الشرين خشية حصول أقواهما. ويتحلى بمكارم الأخلاق ومعالى الشِّيَم،

فيكون ظاهره جميلاً، وباطنه أجمل من ظاهره. وسريرته خيرًا من علانيته، فيزاحم أصحاب المعالى عليها كما يتزاحم أهل الدينار والدرهم عليهما. فبهذه اليقظة يستعد للنوعين الآخرين منهما.

أحدهما: يقظه تبعثه على اقتباس الحياة الدائمة الباقية، التى لا خَطَرَ لها، من هذه الحياة الزائلة الفانية، التى لا قيمة لها.

فإن قلت: مثِّل لى، كيف تقتبسُ الحياة الدائمة من الحياة الفانية؟ وكيف يكون هذا؟ فإنى لا أفهمه.

قلت: وهذا أيضًا من نوم القلب، بل من موته. وهل تقتبس الحياة الدائمة إلا من هذه الحياة الزائلة؟ وأنت قد تشعل سراجك من سراج آخر قد أشفى على الانطفاء، فيتَّقِد الثانى ويضىء غاية الإضاءة، ويتصل ضوءه، وينطفئُ الأول. والمقتبس لحياته الدائمة من حياته المنقطعة: إنما ينتقل من دار منقطعة إلى دار باقية، وقد توسط الموت بين الدارين. فهو قنطرة لا يعبر إلى تلك الدار إلا عليها، وباب لا يدخل إليها إلا منه. فهما حياتان فى دارين بينهما موت؛ وكما أن نور تلك الدار مقتبس من نور هذه الدار، فحياتها كذلك مقتبسة من حياتها. فعلى قدر نور الإيمان فى هذه الدار يكون نور العبد فى تلك الدار. وعلى قدر حياته فى هذه الدار تكون حياته هناك.

نعم هذا النور والحياة، الذى يقتبس منه ذلك النور والحياة، لا ينقطع. بل يضىء للعبد فى البرزخ، وفى موقف القيامة، وعلى الصراط. فلا يفارقه إلى دار الحيوان. يطفأ نور الشمس وهذا النور لا يطفأ. وتبطل الحياة المحسوسة وهذه الحياة لا تبطل. هذا أحد نوعى يقظة القلب.

النوع الثانى: يقظة تبعث على حياة. لا تدركها العبارة. ولا ينالها التوهم. ولا يطابق فيها اللفظ لمعناه ألبتة. والذى يشار به إليها: حياة المحب مع حبيبه، الذى لا قوام لقلبه

وروحه وحياته إلا به ولا غنى له عنه طرفة عين. ولا قرة لعينه، ولا طمأنينة لقلبه، ولا سكون لروحه، إلا به، فهو أحوج إليه من سمعه وبصره وقُوته، بل ومن حياته. فإن حياته بدونه بدون عذاب وآلام، وهموم وأحزان. فحياته موقوفة على قربه وحبه ومصاحبته. وعذاب حجابه عنه: أعظم من العذاب الآخر. كما أن نعيم القلب والروح بإزالة ذلك الحجاب: أعظم من النعيم بالأكل والشرب، والتمتع بالحور العين. فهكذا عذاب الحجاب أعظم من عذاب الجحيم، ولهذا جمع الله سبحانه لأوليائه بين النعيمين فى قوله: ﴿للذين أحسنوا الحسنى وزيادة﴾ [يونس/٢٦] فالحسنى الجنة. والزيادة: رؤية وجهه الكريم فى جنات عدن. وجمع لأعدائه بين العذابين فى قوله: ﴿كلا إنهم عن ربهم يومئذ لمحجوبون * ثم إنهم لصالوا الجحيم﴾ [المطففين/ ١٥،١٦].

والمقصود: أن الغفلة هى نوم القلب عن طلب هذه الحياة. وهى حجاب عليه. فإن كُشف هذا الحجاب بالذكر وإلا تكاثف حتى يصير حجاب بطالة ولعب، واشتغال بما لا يفيد. فإن بادر إلى كشفه، وإلا تكاثف حتى يصير حجاب معاص وذنوب صغار تبعده عن الله. فإن بادر إلى كشفه وإلا تكاثف حتى يصير حجاب كبائر توجب مَقْتَ الرب تعالى له، وغضبه ولعنته. فإن بادر إلى كشفه، وإلا تكاثف حتى صار حجاب بدع عملية يعذب العامل فيها نفسه. ولا تجدى عليه شيئًا. فإن بادر إلى كشفه، وإلا تكاثف حتى صار حجاب بدع قولية اعتقادية. تتضمن الكذب على الله ورسوله ﷺ، والتكذيب بالحق الذى جاء به الرسول ﷺ. فإن بادر إلى كشفه وإلا تكاثف حتى صار حجاب شك وتكذيب. يقدح فى أصول الإيمان الخمسة. (وهى: الإيمان بالله، وملائكته، وكتبه، ورسله، ولقائه) فلغلظ حجابه وكثافته، وظلمته وسواده: لا يرى حقائق الإيمان. ويتمكن منه الشيطان، يَعِدُهُ ويُمنّيه، والنفس الأمارة بالسوء تهوى وتشتهى. وسلطان الطبع قد ظفر بسلطان الإيمان. فأسره وسجنه، إن لم يهلكه. وتولى تدبير المملكة واستخدام جنود الشهوات، وأقطعها العوائد التى جرى عليها العمل. وأغلق باب اليقظة. وأقام عليه بواب الغفلة. وقال: إياك أن نؤتّى من قبلك. واتخذ حاجبًا من الهوى، وقال: إياك أن تمكن أحدًا يدخل علىّ إلا معك. فأمرُ هذه المملكة قد صار إليك وإلى البواب. فيا بواب الغفلة، ويا حاجب الهوى ليلزم كل منكما ثغره، فإن أخليتما فَسَدَ أمر مملكتنا، وعادت الدولة لغيرنا، وسامنا سلطان الإيمان شر الخزى والهوان. ولا نفرح بهذه المدينة أبدًا.

فلا إله إلا الله! إذا اجتمعت على القلب هذه العساكر، مع رِقَّةِ الإيمان، وقلة الأعوان، والإعراض عن ذكر الرحمن، والانخراط فى سلك أبناء الزمان، وطول الأمل المفسد للإنسان - أن آثر العاجل الحاضر على الغائب الموعود به بعد طَيّ هذه الأكوان. فالله المستعان وعليه التكلان.

---

(١) منازل السائرين (ص/٤١) ويقصد بالتى لها ثلاثة أنفاس: الدرجة الأولى من منزلة الحياة وهى (حياة العلم من موت الجهل) كما تقدم ذكر ذلك.

فهذا فصل مختصر نافع في ذكر الحياة وأنواعها، والتشويق إلى أشرفها وأطيبها، فمن صادف من قلبه حياة انتفع به، وإلا فَخُودٌ تزف إلى ضرير مقعد.

فلنرجع إلى شرح كلام صاحب «المنازل»:

* قال: «ولها ثلاثة أنفاس: نفس الخوف، ونفس الرجاء، ونفس المحبة»(١).

لما كان كل حيوان متنفسًا، فإن النفس موجب الحياة وعلامتها: كانت أنفاس الحياة المشار إليها ثلاثة أنفاس:

* نفس الخوف: (ومصدره: مطالعة الوعيد)، وما أعد الله لمن آثر الدنيا على الآخرة.

والمخلوق على الخالق، والهوى على الهدى، والغي على الرشاد.

* ونفس الرجاء: (ومصدره: مطالعة الوعد)، وحسن الظن بالرب تعالى. وما الله أعد لمن آثر الله ورسوله ﷺ، والدار الآخرة، وحكَّمَ الهدى على الهوى، والوحي على الآراء، والسنة على البدعة، وما كان عليه رسول الله ﷺ وأصحابه على عوائد الخلق.

* ونفس بالمحبة: (مصدره: مطالعة الأسماء والصفات، ومشاهدة النعماء والآلاء).

فإذا ذكر ذنوبه: تنفس بالخوف. وإذا ذكر رحمة ربه، وسعة مغفرته وعفوه: تنفس بالرجاء. وإذا ذكر جماله وجلاله وكماله وإحسانه وإنعامه: تنفس بالحب.

فليزن العبد إيمانه بهذه الأنفاس الثلاثة. ليعلم ما معه من الإيمان، فإن القلوب مفطورة على حب الجمال والإجمال. والله سبحانه جميل. بل له الجمال التام الكامل من جميع الوجوه - جمال الذات، وجمال الصفات، وجمال الأفعال، وجمال الأسماء - وإذا جمع جمال المخلوقات كله على شخص واحد، ثم كانت جميعها على جمال ذلك الشخص، ثم نسب هذا الجمال إلى جمال الرب تبارك وتعالى: كان أقل من نسبة سراج ضعيف إلى عين الشمس.

فالنفَس الصادر عن هذه الملاحظة والمطالعة: أشرف أنفاس العبد على الإطلاق. فأين نفس المشتاق المحب الصادق إلى نفس الخائف الراجي؟

ولكن لا يحصل له هذا النفَس إلا بتحصيل ذينك النفسين، فإن أحدهما ثمرة ترك للمخالفات. والثاني: ثمرة فعله للطاعات، فمن هذين النفسين يصل إلى النفس الثالث.

---

(١) منازل السائرين (ص/٤١) ويقصد بالتي لها ثلاثة أنفاس: الدرجة الأولى من منزلة الحياة وهي (حياة العلم من موت الجهل) كما تقدم ذكر ذلك.

فصل [الحياة الثانية : حياة الجمع]

قال: «الحياة الثانية: حياة الجمع من موت التفرقة. ولها ثلاثة أنفاس: نفس الاضطرار، ونفس الافتقار، ونفس الافتخار»[1].

ومراده - إن شاء الله - بالجمع في هذه الدرجة: جمع القلب على الله، وجمع الخواطر والعزوم في التوجه إليه سبحانه. لا الجمع الذي هو حضرة الوجود؛ لأنه قد ذكر حياة هذا الجمع في الدرجة الثالثة. وسماها «حياة الوجود».

وإنما كان جمع القلب على الله والخواطر على السير إليه: حياة حقيقية؛ لأن القلب لا سعادة له، ولا فلاح ولا نعيم، ولا فوز ولا لذة، ولا قرة عين إلا بأن يكون الله وحده هو غاية طلبه، ونهاية قصده. ووجهه الأعلى: هو كل بغيته. فالتفرقة المتضمنة للإعراض عن التوجه إليه، واجتماع القلب عليه: هي مرضه إن لم يمت منها.

٭ قال «ولهذه الحياة ثلاثة أنفاس: نفس الاضطرار»: وذلك لانقطاع أمله مما سوى الله.

فيضطر حينئذٍ - بقلبه وروحه ونفسه وبدنه - إلى ربه ضرورة تامة. بحيث يجد في كل منبت شعرة منه فاقة تامة إلى ربه ومعبوده. فهذا النفس نفس مضطر إلى ما لا غنى له عنه طرفة عين. وضرورته إليه من جهة كونه ربه، وخالقه وفاطره وناصره، وحافظه ومعينه ورازقه، وهاديه ومعافيه، والقائم بجميع مصالحه. ومن جهة كونه: معبوده وإلهه، وحبيبه الذي لا تكمل حياته ولا تنفع إلا بأن يكون هو وحده أحب شيء إليه، وأشوق شيء إليه. وهذا الاضطرار: هو اضطرار «إياك نعبد» والاضطرار الأول: اضطرار «إياك نستعين».

٭ ولعمر الله إن «نفس الافتقار»: هو هذا النفس، أو من نوعه. ولكن الشيخ جعلهما نفسين. فجعل «نفس الاضطرار» بداية، و«نفس الافتقار» توسط، و«نفس الافتخار» نهاية. وكأن «نفس الاضطرار» يقطع الخلق من قلبه، و«نفس الافتقار» يعلق قلبه بربه.

والتحقيق: أنه نفس واحد ممتد. أوله انقطاع. وآخره اتصال.

٭ وأما «نفس الافتخار»: فهو نتيجة هذين النفسين؛ لأنهم إذا صحّا للعبد حصل له القرب من ربه، والأنس به، والفرح به، وبالخلع التي خلعها ربه على قلبه وروحه مما لا يقوم لبعضه ممالك الدنيا بحذافيرها. فحينئذٍ يتنفس نفساً آخر. يجد به من التفريج والترويح والراحة والانشراح ما يشبه - من بعض الوجوه - بنفس مَنْ جُعل في عنقه حبل ليخنق به حتى يموت. ثم كشف عنه وقد حبس نفسه. فتنفس نفس من أعيدت عليه حياته. وتخلص من أسباب الموت.

---

(١) المنازل (ص/ ٤١).

فإن قلت: ما للعبد والافتخار؟ وأين العبودية من نفس الافتخار؟.

قلت: لا يريد بذلك: أن العبد يفتخر بذلك. ويختال على بنى جنسه بل هو فرح وسرور لا يمكن دفعه عن نفسه بما فتح عليه ربه. ومنحه إياه، وخصه به. وأولى ما فرح به العبد: فضل ربه عليه. فإنه تعالى يحب أن يرى أثر نعمته على عبده. ويحب الفرح بذلك؛ لأنه من الشكر. ومن لا يفرح بنعمة المنعم لا يعد شكوراً. فهو افتخار بما هو محض منة الله ونعمته على عبده، لا افتخار بما من العبد. فهذا هو الذى ينافى العبودية لا ذاك.

وهنا سر لطيف: وهو أن هذا النفس يفخر على أنفاسه التى ليست كذلك. كما تفخر الحياة على الموت، والعلم على الجهل، والسمع على الصمم، والبصر على العمى. فيكون الافتخار للنفس على النفس، لا للتنفس على الناس. والله أعلم.

فصل [الحياة الثالثة : حياة الوجود]

قال: «الحياة الثالثة: (حياة الوجود). وهي حياة بالحق. ولها ثلاثة أنفاس: نفس الهيبة (وهو يميت الاعتدال)، ونفس الوجود (وهو يمنع الانفصال)، ونفس الانفراد (وهو يورث الاتصال). وليس وراء ذلك ملحظ للنظارة. ولا طاقة للإشارة»[1].

هذه المرتبة - من الحياة - هي حياة الواجد. وهي أكمل من النوعين اللذين قبلها. ووجود العبد لربه: هو الذي أشار إليه في الحديث الإلهي بقوله: «فإذا أحببته كنت سمعه الذي يسمع به، وبصره الذي يبصر به، ويده التي يبطش بها، ورجله التي يمشي بها. فبي يسمع. وبي يبصر. وبي يبطش. وبي يمشي»[1] والمشار إليه في قوله: «ابنَ آدم، اطلبني تجدني. فإن وجدتني وجدت كل شيء وإن فتُّك فاتك كل شيء».

وسيأتي في باب «الوجود» مزيد لهذا إن شاء الله تعالى.

● [حياة الوجود أكمل الحياة]

وإنما كانت حياة الوجود أكمل الحياة، لشرفها وكمالها بموجدها. وهو الحق سبحانه وتعالى، فمن حُبِي بوجوده فقد فاز بأعلى أنواع الحياة.

فإن قلت: يصعب عليّ فهم معنى الحياة بوجوده.

قلت: لأجل الحجاب الذي ضرب بينك وبين هذه الحياة. فافهم الحياة بوجود الفناء، وبوجود المالك القادر إذا كان معك وناصرك، دون مجرد وجوده - ولا معرفة بينك وبينه ألبتة - فحقيقة الحياة: هي الحياة بالرب تعالى، لا الحياة بالنفس والفناء وأسباب العيش.

✻ وقد تفسر «حياة الوجود»: بشهود القيومية، حيث لا يرى شيئًا من الأشياء إلا وهو بالله. وهو الذي أقامه. وبحال هذا الشهود. وهو أن لا يلتفت بقلبه إلى شيء سوى الله. ولا يخافه ولا يرجوه. بل قد قصر خوفه ورجاءه، وتوكله وإنابته على الحي القيوم، قيوم الوجود وقيِّمه وقيامه ومقيمه وحده. فمتى حصل له هذا الشهود وهذا الحال: فقد حصلت له حياة الوجود.

✻ فتارة يـ «تنفس بالهيبة»: وهي سطوة نور الصفات. وذلك عند أول ما يسطع نور الوجود. فيقع القلب في هيبة تستغرق حسه عن الالتفات إلى شيء من عوالم النفس. وذلك هو الاعتلال الذي يميته النَفَس الثاني. وهو قوله «ونفس يميت الاعتدال» فتموت منه علل أعماله، وآثار حظوظه، وشهود إنيته.

---

(١) منازل السائرين (ص/ ٤١) وفيه: «وهو يميت الاعتلال».

(١) [صحيح] تقدم تخريجه قريبًا.

* قوله «ونفس الوجود»: يريد به: وجود العبد بربه. فيتنفس بهذا الوجود. كما يسمع به، ويبصر به، ويبطش به. ويمشى به.

ولا تصغ إلى غير هذا. فتزل قدم بعد ثبوتها.

* قوله «وهو يمنع الانفصال»: الانفصال عند القوم: انقطاع القلب عن الرب وبقاؤه بنفسه وطبيعته. و«الاتصال» هو بقاؤه بربه، وفناؤه عن أحكام نفسه، وطبعه وهواه.

وقد يراد «بالاتصال» الفناء فى شهود القيومية. و«بالانفصال» الغيبة عن هذا الشهود.

وأما الملحد: فيفسر «الاتصال، والانفصال» بالاتصال الذاتى والانفصال الذاتى. وهذا محال أيضًا. فإنه لم يزل متصلًا به. بل لم يزل إياه عنده.

فالأول: يتعلق بالإرادة والهمة. وهو أعلى الأنواع.

والثانى: يتعلق بالشهود والشعور. وهو دونه. وهو عند الشيخ أعلى؛ لأنه إنما يكون فى وادى الفناء.

والثالث: للملاحدة القائلين بوحدة الوجود.

* قوله «ونفس الانفراد. وهو يورث الاتصال»:

نفس الانفراد: هو المصحوب بشهود الفردانية. وهى تفرد الرب سبحانه بالربوبية والإلهية، والتدبير والقيومية. فلا يثبت لسواه قسطًا فى الربوبية، ولا يجعل لسواه حظًا فى الإلهية، ولا فى القيومية. بل يفرده بذلك فى شهوده، كما أفرده به فى علمه، ثم يفرده به فى الحال التى أوجبها له الشهود. فيكون الله سبحانه فردًا فى علم العبد ومعرفته، فردًا فى شهوده، فردًا فى حاله فى شهوده.

وهذا النفس يورثه الاتصال بربه، بحيث لا يبقى له مراد غيره، ولا إرادة غير مراده الدينى الذى يحبه ويرضاه. فيستفرغ حبه قلبه. وتستفرغ مرضاته سعيه، وليس وراء ذلك مقام يلحظه النظارة، لا بالقلب ولا بالروح.

فإن كمال هذا الاتصال، والشغل بالحق سبحانه: قد استفرغ المقامات، واستوعب الإشارات. والله المستعان.